NO CHILD
LEFT
UNWRAPPED

Understanding
and Honoring
the Gifts
Every Child is
Born With

For Rev Lawrence
May your Gifts be
unwrapped and
shared with the
world.

Shelley L. Francis

This book reflects my present recollections of experiences over time. While all the stories in this book are true, some names and identifying details have been changed to protect the privacy of individuals. In some cases, events have been combined.

Publishing Services provided by Paper Raven Books

Printed in the United States of America

First Printing, 2018

Paperback ISBN= 978-1-7326477-0-1
Hardback ISBN= 978-1-7326477-1-8

I dedicate this book to all the children who I have been blessed to work with over the years and who have taught me more than I could have ever imagined.

I dedicate this book to my mother and all the other parents who have suffered not understanding their child's different ways of processing the world.

And lastly, I dedicate this book to my brother, Tommy, my greatest teacher, whose lifelong challenges have been my greatest motivator. I have had a front row seat to the heartache that comes from watching a family member struggle with finding their place in a world that just doesn't fit their beautiful heart. When beautiful gifts remain hidden, it's not just the child who suffers, but all of humanity misses out on the blessings that are meant to be unwrapped, cultivated, and ultimately shared.

TABLE OF CONTENTS

FOREWORD

I met Shelley Francis in 2015 as one of my coaching students.

I was immediately struck not only by her intelligence, deep skillset, and wisdom but also by her ingrained dedication and compassion to support the many special sensitive children who require our attention in a new way.

There is an evolutionary change happening on our beautiful blue planet. More and more children are being born with what appears to be gifts of a deep sensitivity. I believe they are here to help make a change to all aspects of humanity that we desperately require.

The old "diagnoses" of autism, dyslexia, ADHD, auditory processing and learning disabilities, etc., may not be symptoms of something wrong, but may actually be providing us with a new perspective illustrating a way to contribute healing to the world and ourselves.

What is needed now is not a way to "fix" these children, but instead to understand them, leverage their great gifts, and support them in showing us what is possible now in a new paradigm of compassion and sensitivity.

The world is in true need of more caring and compassionate people. I believe that these sensitive children are here to provide that. However, the old societal paradigm, social norms, and outdated educational paradigms do not provide what these beautiful children require.

Instead, they are poked and prodded and told they have "disabilities."

In this book, Shelley will reveal how we can not only support these children but also bring out the best of their natural and unique gifts. Shelley's idea is that there are physical senses and inner senses, and as a society we are entirely too focused on the external and developing the physical senses.

Here, you will not only learn how to connect and develop the inner senses but also why this is so important especially for sensitive children. Their heart and inner senses are their gifts, and they need to be cultivated and nurtured.

Be prepared to receive insights, techniques, and research that illustrate a new paradigm that honors children's sensitivity and helps them to develop their inner senses.

As someone who was diagnosed with ADHD and dyslexia, I had to figure it out on my own. I didn't really understand the gift in these labels and how to actually use them to create a successful business and happy life. Growing up, the focus was on the challenges that these gifts presented. I wish there was someone there for me who could have demonstrated how these challenges were actually my superpowers.

I don't want this next generation of children to move through life in fear and confusion as I did. I don't want them to wait until later in life as I had to. I was in my 40s before I figured it out.

I'm delighted you have this book in your hands now, and I know it will help you support the children in your life to be happy and to develop and cultivate their gifts.

I can't think of a better, more knowledgeable and compassionate person to guide you than Shelley Francis. You are in good hands.

Jennifer McLean
Author, Healer, CEO,
Creator of the Spontaneous Transformation
Technique
October 11, 2018

INTRODUCTION

When I was a child, I witnessed a tornado. I recall huddling up with my mother and my brother while we listened to the radio give an account of a storm that was in our vicinity and producing tornados all around us. Suddenly, the radio went dead and the power turned off. We headed downstairs as the sky turned a greenish-gray color, and we heard what sounded like a freight train heading straight for us. The sound got louder and louder until all at once it was quiet. Once the storm had ended, the day turned into one of the most beautiful days I have ever seen. The rain was gone, the sky was blue, and the air smelled so fresh. The horrible noise had disappeared, and there was a peacefulness in the quiet. I recall in that moment that the world seemed so beautiful, so calm. Then we became aware of the sirens, and with the curious eyes of children, my brother and I hopped on our bikes and rode off to explore what was going on. Just a few blocks away, we were amazed to see the destruction that had taken place so close to our own pristine home. A tornado had touched down, destroying a community in front of us and then another one behind us. I noticed that although the fronts of the homes were gone, the furniture remained intact. They looked like life-size doll houses, a vision that has remained with me throughout my life. I have always been in wonderment of this experience and how a tornado could pull the front of a building off from its foundation and yet not disturb the furniture inside.

Today, I see how life and the world around us can be so very challenging, and at the same time, within each of us, there is a beautiful gift of resilience. We don't always recognize it is there, because most of us spend much of our life focused on outside forces and circumstances, but within each of us lies our true gift. The outside storms of our life will shape and mold us, and we may even feel as if it will break us at times. But inside of each of us lives a resilient, loving soul who knows the truth of who we are. During times of need, we all seem to be able to come together and support each other. When our heart appears to be breaking, there is a hidden force that is present, connecting each of us with compassion and empathy.

We come into this world with a body that is the home to our spirit. Immediately, our body begins making connections through our senses, and over time we grow and develop a healthy strong relationship with our physical world. As parents, doctors, and teachers, we are extremely focused on watching our children meet certain developmental milestones, and we are ready to jump in and provide extra help if it looks like a child is lagging behind one or more of these markers. But what about a child's inner world, their spirit and true essence? From an early age, this inner knowing of who we are often gets lost or hidden behind what we think we should be, or told who we are.

Events such as September 11th, school shootings, and natural disasters have all shown us how our true compassion for one another is always there, ready to provide support in times of need. This is the power of the heart, our true inner knowing of who we are and that we are all connected. In our day-to-day lives, however, we often neglect this part of us, because we are so attached to our external programming and outer circumstances that we forget who we really are. The storms of our life will create and shape our outer world, but at our core, each of us has a resilient heart that is the true essence of who we are. Navigating through our life's challenges and struggles can certainly make us all stop and wonder why things have to be so hard. But when it comes to our children, it can be extremely difficult to make sense out of it all. It's one thing to face these challenges ourselves, but it is extremely difficult to watch our children go through these challenges.

We feel a sense of responsibility to make sure our children are happy. We believe that it is our job to pave the road of success for them so that they may find their way through life. We want to clear the road of all debris, road blocks, speed bumps, and pot holes. We want our children to stand tall and shine. We want others to look at our children with kindness and love. We want to clear the way of all the clutter, all the negativity, and all the heartache and suffering that often comes with life. We believe that it is our job to make sure they are happy and that they grow up healthy, strong, with a good sense of self. When our children suffer, we suffer. When our children hurt, we hurt. When our children are not happy, we are not happy.

When a child is born, a parent is filled with joy and dreams of a healthy, happy child growing up to be a healthy, happy adult. We imagine all the wonderful events that we will experience with our children. We imagine the joy in their faces when they meet Mickey Mouse for the first time. We imagine their happiness and sense of accomplishment when they take their first steps, when they say their first words, and when they read their first book. We imagine them coming home from school, happy and proud of all they have learned that day. We look forward to watching our children play and build friendships with other children.

But what happens when the joys we are looking forward to don't turn out the way we planned? When instead of running up and hugging Mickey Mouse, they are so frightened that they hide behind you, grabbing onto your leg, digging their fingernails into the flesh of your thigh. When instead of being excited to go to school, they cry and scream that they do not want to go. When instead of coming home with friends to play with, they come home crying that the other children have been making fun of them. When instead of being proud of what they have accomplished in school, they call themselves stupid.

When our children have these experiences, we do too, and this can leave us feeling overwhelmed, frightened, angry, lost, and hopeless. We feel a sense of responsibility for our child's life, and with this comes a need to control the circumstances surrounding their challenges. We search for answers. We look for solutions. We spend countless hours and sleepless nights on Google searches and Facebook chats. We talk to anyone and everyone that might give us a little guidance, and often, we are left feeling more overwhelmed and more confused. The storm of our lives seems to be building momentum, with little or no end in sight. We ask ourselves, "Why is this happening to us? Why is this happening to my child?" Have you cried yourself to sleep wondering what was going to become of your child? Do you wake up in the morning wondering what storm you are going to face today? Have you prayed for answers? Do you want to cry out, "SOMEONE, PLEASE HELP ME!"?

As a parent, I know what it feels like to experience your child's ups and downs right along with them. And as an audiologist who has worked with children for most of my career, I know that we as professionals can easily get overwhelmed when we cannot figure out how to help a particular child. We choose these careers, because we want to make a difference in the life of a child, but when we struggle with accomplishing this, we can easily feel discouraged and get caught up in placing the blame on outer circumstances over which we have no control. It is easy to get wrapped up in our own mind, thinking about all the things we have learned in school or from society about how to best serve our children, but we often lose sight of who these children truly are at their core. When we get lost in our thinking about how to serve them, we often lose touch with our heart and our inner knowing of what they truly need.

True happiness is our birth right, and the road to true happiness is authenticity. Our real journey lies within. Getting to know our true nature and being able to make peace with ourselves is the key. My own life continues to lead me on a journey of self-discovery. Every challenge that I have faced has made me who I am today. When I look back on my life, I can see how every hurdle I overcame, and every hardship I endured, was perfectly placed at the right time.

My career as an audiologist began with a desire that I had always had to work with children. However, during my last semester in my audiology graduate program, I was presented with an opportunity to do one of my clinical placements in a hearing aid office. At the time, I told my professor that I did not have any desire to work in a hearing aid office, so it would probably be better if I could have another placement in a hospital or school instead. He responded by encouraging me to take the opportunity to see what a private practice audiology setting was like. I took his advice, and at the end of the semester, right before I graduated, the owner of the practice offered me a job there. One of his audiologists was going on maternity leave, and he needed someone for at least a year. So, I took the job, feeling very happy that I had a job before I graduated. When the audiologist I had replaced came back to work, I was offered several positions in the Dallas, Texas area, where I was living at the time. One day, I received a phone call from a company offering me a position in New York, running one of their 40 hearing aid offices.

I remember thinking that I definitely did not want to move from Texas to New York, but for some reason, my mouth said yes, and within two weeks I was living in Long Island, New York running a fairly busy hearing aid office. Moving to New York from Texas certainly had its own unique challenges, but the biggest challenge came about 18 months after making the move, when I received a federal express letter at work on a Saturday morning that the company had filed for bankruptcy, and I had two weeks to pack up the office and find a new job. This was certainly a shocker that left me with some big decisions to make. Do I go back to Texas to be close to family and look for a new job, or do I look for a job in New York? I had bills to pay and no source of income outside of the two-week window I was given. This apparent challenge turned out to be the greatest blessing in my professional career. I ended up going to the bankruptcy court to buy my patients' files and all the equipment I needed for a hundred dollars, renting a space three blocks away, and starting my own private practice. However, this was a hearing aid practice, and remember, I always wanted to work with children, so what happened next was another gift.

I grew up in a small family with a single mom and a brother with an undiagnosed learning disability. My brother's challenges learning and my mother's challenges trying to understand and help him played a significant role in my career after I started my private practice. I began seeing more and more children who were coming in for hearing tests, because their parents or teachers had concerns about their ability to listen. As I saw more and more of these children, I began to notice that they seemed to have some of the same challenges that my brother had.

I started exploring a topic that I did not learn about in school and that was extremely controversial within the audiology community at the time. That topic was central auditory processing disorder. I was deeply fascinated by it, and I could not get my hands on enough reading material. I read whatever I could find (which wasn't much), and I began exploring people like Jean Ayres and her work with sensory integration. Before I knew it, my hearing aid practice had transformed into an audiology practice specializing in the diagnosis and treatment of auditory processing disorder, and yes, you guessed it, most of my patients were children.

Challenges watching my brother and my mother struggle as I was growing up, then challenges I faced moving away from my friends and family and ultimately losing my place of employment, were the storms in my life that led me on a journey toward a career that I love. The children I have been honored to work with, and the parents who have come to me throughout the years for help, have taught me more than I ever could have imagined. My work with families has taught me the greatest truth: *your child is not broken, and they do not need to be fixed.* They are perfect exactly the way they are. God does not make mistakes. The life journey that they are on is the perfect storm. It is not your job to fix them. Just love them, and accept them for who they are and for the gifts they bring to this world. Now, that doesn't mean we don't want to help them. It just means that helping them may look a little different than it has in the past. Every child is born into this world with special gifts that are meant to be shared. Every child is a genius. As Albert Einstein once said, "If you judge a fish by the way he climbs a tree, he will spend his entire life believing he is stupid."

This does not mean, however, that we just sit back and do nothing. What I am suggesting is that we just take a deeper look into the messages being sent to us. There is more than meets the eye. Today, there are more and more children struggling. Many are struggling to learn, many are struggling with knowing who they are, and many are struggling with just trying to fit in. The modern world offers more external challenges for children to navigate. The internet, for example, is a beautiful tool that has the power to connect us with people all over the world and allow us to learn and grow from each other. However, it also has the power to be a vehicle of bullying and of emotional abuse. Its gift is that it can help us all come together, but its curse is that it can also be misused in a way that can cause separation and isolation.

We are also living in a world that is witnessing many tragic events, both natural and man-made. In this book, we will explore how children today are impacted by these events on an elevated level. Children today feel these events stronger and deeper than ever before. They are facing tremendous change in the world, not just from external sources but also from internal changes, and in order to help them, we have to look beyond the external events and begin to focus on the inner experiences. Humanity's resilience can be witnessed if we look beyond what we see and hear and pay attention to the changes that are happening within our children. The world is filled with challenges and obstacles, for we are all witnessing the perfect storm, and our children hold the key to humanity's survival. But to find this key, it will be necessary to look beyond what we have known in the past and to discover the truth that lies within. Yes, our children today are evolving, and we can help them by dismantling our old paradigm and creating a new paradigm that will better serve humanity.

In this book, we will begin in Part One by understanding and discovering how our physical senses connect us with the physical world through childhood development and the impact it has when specific skills lag behind or don't integrate with each other. We will explore language development and the importance of hearing versus listening when it comes to speech and language skills. Next, we will move on to understanding labels and how they can have both a positive and a negative impact on our children. Here, we will go beyond the physical and explore our inner senses and how more and more children today are coming into this world with a heightened ability to connect and maintain their internal senses.

In Part Two, we take a deep look into our belief system and how self-limiting beliefs are formed as well as how they impact us. We discuss the importance of helping our children discover who they truly are without the negative programming from the outside world. We will also explore how the old societal paradigm is no longer serving our children and youth of today, and how we can help them build a strong healthy sense of self. This is followed up with understanding how children today are evolving and how modern-day parenting is supporting an old paradigm. I will demonstrate how our children and youth will greatly benefit from moving toward a more cooperative paradigm from one based in competition.

In Part Three, we will dive deep into the metaphysical. By going beyond the physical, we will begin to understand how children today are evolving and how we can support them during these turbulent times of change. Here is where we will begin to unwrap the gifts every child is born with. This is where we truly understand how every child plays an important role in the evolution of humanity. Understanding and honoring these gifts is vitally important in helping our children lead the way toward a beautiful tomorrow.

Finally, I have included letters from the heart. This is where I hope you will get a chance to truly feel the heart of today's children and the unique challenges they are facing. In reading these, I hope you will experience the courage of not only today's children but also their parents, teachers, and advocates.

I believe humanity is being supported by helping us move from a mind-based paradigm to a heart-based paradigm, and our children are here to support this change. They are being born more sensitive and more caring, with a deep inner way of experiencing the world. However, too many of our children are being lost within our educational system, within society, and within their own self-beliefs. It is my hope that this book will provide insights into how our children today are evolving and how we can best serve them during this turbulent time of change. I truly believe that our children are here to lead the way into a more cooperative and empathic society. Every child is born with beautiful gifts that are meant to be shared with the world, but far too often these gifts remain hidden due to society's beliefs and an old-world paradigm. It is time for us to change this paradigm and allow our children to be who they have come here to be. It is time to unwrap the gifts that every child is born with and allow their true awesomeness to shine and be seen.

GLOSSARY OF TERMS

Extra sensitive or highly sensitive: having a sensory system that is easily stimulated with a lower than normal input

Hypersensitive: a particular sensory area that responds to lower than normal input

Hypo sensitive: a particular sensory area that is less sensitive to normal input and requires a stronger stimulus to receive the information

Sensory sensitive: a person who is easily overstimulated by one or more of their senses

Empath: a person who is able to easily feel what another person is feeling

Neurotypical or neurologically typical: a person who does not have a developmental delay or other neurological difference, often used to describe someone who is not autistic

Neurodivergent: a person who is processing information differently from a neurotypical person; does not necessarily mean autistic, but does include autism and any other neurological differences

Neurodiversity: the opposite of neurotypical, refers to having a sensory processing system that processes information differently than what is typical

Physical senses: the sensory processing system that picks up and organizes stimuli from the outside of the body or from the physical world

Inner senses: our ability to receive and organize information on an energetic level

Inner guidance: our intuition or our ability to be guided by feelings rather than by thought

Inner knowing: the ability to trust what we are feeling as the truth rather than following societal beliefs or what we think is true based on our individual thoughts; can include intuition, creativity, and insight

PART I

A Child's Unique Experience of the Outside World

CHAPTER 1

Unwrapping Senses

*Understanding how senses develop and what
it means to be a sensory child*

For years, I have heard parents describe their child as being "very sensory." With further inquiry, I would find that they were describing their child as being very sensitive to touch, taste, smells, and to the environment in general. But what does sensory really mean? In school, we learned that we have five senses: touch, smell, taste, sight, and hearing. So, what does it mean to say a child is sensory? Aren't we all sensory? Don't we all have, more or less, the same physical senses?

What I have realized is that when parents refer to their child as being sensory, they are usually referring to mostly the sense of touch. They report such things as having to cut the tags out of their child's clothes or put their socks on inside out so they don't feel the seam on their toes. They can't walk on grass or in the sand at the beach. Parents have a difficult time bathing them, because they do not like getting wet or cannot stand to have on wet clothes. Sometimes parents even report that they do not like clothes at all and prefer being naked. Occasionally, they will add that they are very picky eaters, smell everything or don't like smells, and are easily overwhelmed in noisy or crowded places.

What I have come to realize is that being "sensory" means so much more than simply having a heightened sense of touch, taste, smell, sight, or hearing. Quite simply, we are all sensory, for that is an essential part of the human experience. When we come into this world, we experience life from within a human body. This body is the vehicle we will be using throughout our lifetime to connect us with the physical world around us. This connection to our outside world is made through our senses, which includes our central nervous system. The central nervous system is the area in the brain that is responsible for making sense out of the world around us.

By organizing and integrating the information coming in from our different senses, we are able to make good, strong connections with our physical world and to grow and develop a strong healthy relationship with our physical world. This is a natural process that we can observe as we watch our children develop. One connection leads to another connection, which leads to another and another and so on. Each new connection is dependent upon the previous connections in order to develop a good, strong foundation.

We have all heard the saying "you have to walk before you run." Well, that is true. It is very important to learn to walk before you run, as it is just as important to crawl before you walk, creep before you crawl, and roll over before you creep. Each step in the process of learning to walk is just as important as the next step. If you skip steps or quickly go through the steps without an appropriate amount of time to experience each step, it can result in a weak foundation. As important as it is to develop a good foundation, it is equally important to develop integration. Sensory integration is the blending of our different senses in order for them to come together and form a functioning system.

The Senses Working Together

When explaining to parents how the senses work together, I like to use the example of a baby learning to roll over. I had the privilege of witnessing this beautiful experience during my daughter's development when she was three months old. Instinctually, she started pushing down on the floor with one of her arms and rocking back and forth. Now, at that age, it was not her conscious intention to roll over, but it was her instinct that she should be pushing down on the floor. And while she was pushing, she was experiencing the pleasant feeling of rocking back and forth. Let's pretend for a moment that we are this young, newly formed human being experiencing the world in this new and curious way. Rocking is something that we have enjoyed in our parents' arms or in a rocker or a swing, and now we are experiencing this pleasant movement by our own control. So here we are, ahhhhh, gently rocking back and forth, and in the process we are building more and more momentum, when all of a sudden, we roll over onto our backs. Whoa! What was that?!

Let's explore what just happened. By rocking back and forth and gradually picking up momentum, our body suddenly changed positions, and instead of looking at the floor and feeling all the pressure on our stomachs and front of our legs, now we are feeling all of the pressure on our back (sense of touch) and looking up toward the ceiling or at mom's or dad's face staring at us (sense of sight). We also have a new sensation of our spatial awareness, which is a sensory system controlled by our vestibular system that is part of our inner ear. And as if all that wasn't enough, we may also be exposed to the roar of a loud crowd (possibly mom or dad) cheering such things as Yay, you did it! Good job! Wow! What just happened is that several sensory systems experienced a change in sensation all at the same time. This blending of sensory sensations in order to form a functioning whole is also called *sensory integration*. Another way to describe it is *the ability for one sensory system to communicate with another sensory system*. This communication between sensory inputs is essential to the human body for making connections to the physical world.

Like a finely tuned orchestra, one instrument is connected to another and another and another in order to produce a beautiful sound. Like the central nervous system, each of the different instruments are blended together in order to produce a "functioning whole" or, in this case, beautiful music. If any of the instruments are not in tune (foundation) or not in sync with one another (integration), the outcome will not be beautiful music and will instead be a lot of disconnected noise. As with the orchestra that is not in sync and can produce disjointed noise, so can a sensory system that is not integrating properly produce what I like to call *sensory disorganization*. Now, let's break this down a little further by comparing the experiences of Casey and Brady.

Our three-month-old Casey is lying on her belly and pushing instinctually with one of her arms, which creates this gentle rocking back and forth. This pushing action helps to develop the child's sense of *proprioception* or, simply put, feeling of body movement. Now, it starts out instinctual, but as the child experiences this gentle rocking, she may relate this to the soothing sensation of rocking in mommy's arms. This is perceived as a positive event, so she continues to push, which continues the rocking, further developing strength in her upper body that she is going to need when she begins to crawl. In other words, it is further integrating her sense of proprioception (feeling of body movement) with her *vestibular sense* (where she is in space). This natural experience is creating both the foundational skills and the sensory integration skills necessary to walk and move the body through space. These are the early building blocks that will eventually allow this child to walk, run, and play.

Now, let's look at it through the experience of three-month-old Brady. It is Brady's instinct to push, and in doing so he begins to rock. For Brady, rocking has not been a pleasant experience. Brady has a disorganized sensory processing system, and therefore, he is not able to organize the sensory input he is receiving from his different senses. This experience for Brady is a negative one and, subsequently, a scary one. Brady's immediate reaction to the rocking sensation is one of fear, and pushing created the rocking, so he does not continue to push. Brady is not going to roll over today. Eventually, after a while, Brady continues to push a little at a time since it is instinctual, stopping whenever he experiences the fear. Slowly, he becomes stronger, and eventually, one day, he pushes himself over.

YIKES! If Brady was frightened by the rocking movement, you can just imagine how scary it must be to roll over for the first time. His back hitting the floor may have felt like getting hit by a two-by-four. The new visual landscape may leave him feeling as if he has just jetted off to a foreign country. His vestibular system and spatial awareness may have him feeling as if he is floating out in outer space somewhere. Not to mention how the hoots and hollers from his audience with his hypersensitive hearing sounds like he landed smack down in the middle of a Dallas Cowboy football game.

When the sensory processing system is slow to learn to integrate, then these simple experiences can be extremely overwhelming. In this scenario, Brady is not going to want to roll over again anytime soon.

Since rolling over helps to build upper body strength and helps the body learn to integrate its different senses, delaying the experience of rolling over will further delay not only muscle strength and sensory integration but also motor planning. The overall disconnect with the physical world can also lead to fears and anxiety. Eventually, Brady may be diagnosed as being low-toned and may require services such as occupational therapy or physical therapy. Like a fine-tuned orchestra, our sensory system needs to integrate and be in sync together in order to make sense out of this physical world; otherwise, a disconnection in one area can create disorganization that leads to a number of delays and challenges throughout development.

Children with disorganized sensory processing systems can learn the foundational and integration skills necessary for development, but it requires creating an environment conducive to their learning needs. One of my patients Matt was diagnosed as being on the autism spectrum with low tone, obsessive-compulsive disorder, and anxiety disorder. At the time, Matt was five years old. During a listening session, he was rolled back from a sitting-up position to lying on his back. At the moment his position changed, a look of fright came over his face, and his legs and arms spread out quickly in a protective reflex. Matt immediately changed from laughing and having fun to being extremely frightened and completely withdrawn. Due to his disorganized sensory processing system, the change in position gave him a very negative experience, so he avoided it in his everyday activities at every cost, even if it meant that he would be labeled or judged as being defiant.

Knowing that Matt really liked to play and had a connection with a particular therapist, we set up a game where if he rolled back a little, he would be rewarded by this person making a silly face and giving him a puzzle piece. Over the period of about 15 minutes, Matt began to roll back farther and farther, playing and giggling the entire time until eventually he was able to roll back completely. The next day when the game was attempted again, there was a slight hesitance due to his previously learned fear, but he quickly transitioned into the fun game remembering the positive experience he'd had the day before. His old, fearful experience was able to be replaced by a new, pleasant experience.

Brain plasticity research has shown us that we can change the way the brain processes information; in fact, isn't that all development is? By engaging in a fun, rewarding activity over and over again, new neural pathways are formed. We can change an old negative pattern, but only if we override the fear with an outcome that is positive and engaging. As with Casey who continued to roll over because the result was fun and engaging, so, too, did Matt change his negative pattern, because the fun was greater than the fear and he was in an environment that he trusted.

A child with a disorganized sensory processing system learns that they cannot trust the world around them, and therefore, in an attempt to protect themselves, they develop certain behaviors and controls in order to survive in their scary world. Bearing this in mind, we can see how a child like Matt may have developed the behaviors that were later diagnosed as obsessive-compulsive disorder and anxiety disorder. Our sensory system needs to integrate and be in sync together in order to make sense out of the physical world. One of the primary ways senses develop in children is through play.

Sensory Development through Play

Childhood development occurs through play. A child plays because it is fun or because there is some kind of perceived benefit, and through this play, a child strengthens the processing system by building strong foundations and a cohesive integration system. The result is a well-developed sensory processing system. There are two types of play that support different types of development: physical play supports physical development, and creative play supports inner development. *Physical play* connects and develops our physical senses with the external environment, and is an essential part of physical development. For example, throwing or kicking a ball helps to develop and integrate the visual system with the proprioceptive system and helps to develop hand-eye coordination. Climbing, swinging, and sliding are all activities that will help to integrate the vestibular system, the proprioceptive system, and the visual system. As long as a child is successful and is having fun, they will continue to participate in the activity, which will help in developing these particular senses as well as integrate these senses with each other.

Nonphysical, or creative, play is also important to connect and develop the inner senses. Through creative play, a child can use their imagination, which is one way of strengthening the inner senses. When I was a child much of my play was creative. My friends and I were always creating new ways to entertain ourselves, since there was little structure in play activities back then. We created our own games and used things we would find in creative ways. Games like kick the can, rocks, and schoolhouse were ways in which we would spend our time and create new worlds using our imaginations.

Today, children participate in so many scheduled and organized activities that there is little time for creative play. However, it is important to find the balance of both creative play and physical play, especially since creative play can help develop the physical senses. For example, coloring, art projects, and building with Legos are all forms of creative play, which also help to develop fine motor skills and coordination, and develop and organize their physical senses. If a child has weak fine motor skills and loves trains, you can motivate them in improving their fine motor skills by encouraging them and assisting them in building the track. You can help stimulate creative play by encouraging them to come up with their own track design and also by adding houses and other items to the play area. If a child already has strong physical development, you can support creativity development by helping them design and build an obstacle course to jump and climb through. There are endless opportunities when you combine your own imagination along with a good understanding of how play is used in sensory development.

Providing opportunity for both physical and creative play helps develop balance and harmony and is also important for social and emotional development. We can use play for teaching cooperation and the power of working together as opposed to individually. It is also a good way to honor diversity and to demonstrate the importance of having and sharing all different types of talents. For example, I remember watching my daughter play a game at church where all the kids in her class were standing in a circle. One child started the game by throwing a ball of string to another child in the circle while holding onto the loose end of the string. Before they threw the ball of string, they had to say their name and give one interesting fact about themselves. They continued this way, holding the string and throwing the ball, until everyone had a chance to catch the ball, say their name, and tell an interesting fact about themselves. At the end, they were all connected by this intertwined string. This was a fun way for everyone to get to know each other and at the same time exercise their physical bodies, listening skills, and auditory memory.

Listening is another important skill that can be developed through play. I can remember playing many listening games in school, such as Simon Says, Duck Duck Goose, and the Telephone Game, just to name a few. Today, we are in such a rush to teach our children academics that important foundational skills such as listening are getting overlooked and pushed aside. Learning to listen is not only important for academics, but it is also important for social and emotional development. Being a good listener helps in forming friendships and other interpersonal relationships. The need to feel a sense of belonging is vitally important to developing a healthy sense of self. Being able to show empathy by being a good listener will help in developing relationships with others and will therefore contribute to developing a sense of value and of worthiness.

Normal Versus Abnormal Play

The scientific community has determined what is normal play and what is considered abnormal play. We can think of "abnormal" as simply different play from a typical-developing child. We often call this type of play a behavior and, more specifically, a negative behavior. But in fact, it is quite simply play for this specific child within the dynamics of how they are perceiving the world around them. Children play; this is how they develop. From their play, there must be a perceived benefit. As we have seen in the previous examples with Brady and Matt, a child with a disorganized sensory processing system does not receive benefit in the same ways a typically developing child does. Their behavior may be seen as abnormal, but in fact, their behavior may be very normal based on the way they are perceiving the world around them. Let's take a look at different types of play that may appear abnormal but in fact make sense in the context of a disorganized sensory processing system.

**The child who lines everything up.
Everything has a place and that's where
it should be. Everything has to be
completed and has to be put away.**

When the world is perceived as chaotic through a disorganized sensory system, a child's play may reflect this in their need to have everything in a sensible order. This child will find comfort in organizing the chaos. The need to control their environment is evident in the way that they play. Everything has a place, and that is where it should be. When an activity is started, often there is a need to finish it. This completion is a way of maintaining control in an otherwise out-of-control world. A task has a beginning and an end, and its completion helps provide order.

Lining things up in a straight line brings order to a visual system that is not able to make sense out of visual stimuli that appears to have no order. Organizing toys into a straight line allows this child to notice the details of each toy and compare the visual differences of each size, shape, and color. This type of play may bring comfort to this child by allowing them to make a connection with a group of physical objects. With the idea of control in mind, one can easily see how some of these children may develop repetitive behaviors and, in some cases, may be diagnosed with an obsessive-compulsive disorder. So, is it abnormal behavior or a normal response to the world as they see it? Let's look at Nate and how his hypersensitivity was reflected in the way he played. Early on, Nate was very particular about the toys that he would play with when he came to my office. If there was a piece missing to a figurine set or if there was a broken piece, he would get very upset, and we would have to remove that toy or puzzle from the room. He also had a very good memory, and if he returned to the office even months later, he would remember if a particular toy or puzzle had a missing piece and would refuse it.

Nate was also extraordinarily good at doing puzzles. As a child, he was doing three or more 100-piece puzzles in fewer than 30 minutes. As he grew older, he was also able to put these same 100-piece puzzles together upside down without seeing the picture side. It was astounding to watch him put the puzzle together one piece at a time, starting from the top left and going across and down in precise order, while only removing one piece at a time from the box. The fact that he could pick out the correct piece that was the next one in the sequence was simply amazing. Nate would never leave a puzzle unfinished. If he started it, he would not leave until he was given the chance to finish it.

Eventually, Nate was diagnosed with obsessive-compulsive disorder and was placed on medication to help him cope with everyday activities. I still wonder to this day how his life would have turned out differently if his behavior had been seen as needing to be understood instead of seen as needing to be treated. Understanding the why of a behavior gives us a different perception of our children, and a different perception is the first step to helping them.

The child who can't sit still and seems to go from one activity to the next. They appear to be very disorganized, and playtime is rather chaotic.

This child is often referred to as "sensory seeking." They have difficulty focusing on the same task and may play with several things at the same time or quickly jump around from one activity to the next. These children can be exhausting. They are usually very disorganized from their rooms to their overall appearance. Even if they are dressed to perfection for a special occasion, it won't be long before the lived-in look begins to surface. Their desks in school have little to no order, their homework may take them 30 minutes just to organize before they can even begin working on it, and it is usually the parent who has to organize it for them. It is also the parent who has to sit with them and keep them on task, which can be frustrating and exhausting for both parent and child.

However, these are generally the children who are most creative. They are the artists, the musicians, and the storytellers. Their play is generally quite imaginative. They don't need expensive store-bought toys, because they can play with anything. They will create musical instruments with your pots and pans and kitchen tools. They will build a fort out of your cushions and sheets or your empty boxes. You may come home to a kitchen disaster the day they discover they can make their own play dough. You may also find that the toys they do have suddenly acquire a new use. These are also the children who are often diagnosed with attention-deficit/hyperactivity disorder (ADHD) and put on medication.

I remember one little boy I was working with, Stan, who was diagnosed autistic at the age of three. He was nonverbal and extremely active. I remember other parents in my office expressing their concern for his mother. Stan would never sit still and was constantly in motion, often throwing things, and himself, against the wall, furniture, and floor. By the time I had met his mother, she displayed an overwhelming look of hopelessness and despair. She was in search of anything that could possibly help her son. What I remember most about Stan was the remarkable change I saw in him as he got older. With consistent auditory processing therapy as well as occupational therapy, physical therapy, and speech and language therapy, Stan's overall development began to catch up, and he eventually lost the label of autism.

My most joyful recollection was when at the age of eight, he was sitting, completely focused on his drawing. All of a sudden, he jumped out of the chair, threw himself to the floor on his hands and knees, and began screaming "hee haw, hee haw." He was kicking his feet back and up in the air, and I had no idea what this behavior was or what triggered it. Then I looked down to see what he was drawing, and at the young age of eight, Stan had drawn a beautiful picture of Pinocchio turning into a donkey. The picture was amazing, with every detail so clear. I remember the conversation I had with his mom about the event and how she was concerned about this odd behavior and how he was going to survive in this world. I reminded her that there are a lot of amazing people in the world who might be described as eccentric. I often wonder where Stan is today, and I hope that his beautiful gifts are being shared with the world.

Is It Safe to Come Out and Play?

Safety is a basic human need. According to Abraham Maslow's hierarchy of needs as published in his 1943 paper "A Theory of Human Motivation," safety is the second most important instinctual human need next to the physiological needs of human survival, such as breathing, eating, drinking, and sleeping. A child needs to feel safe in their environment. It is quite difficult to feel safe in a world that has no consistency and is continuously unpredictable. Think about it. Since we connect with the physical world through our sensory system, if our sensory system is giving us mixed information, then the physical world that we are living in will not feel safe. Instead, this world will seem quite frightening.

Since safety is a primary need, a child's play must be perceived as safe. Therefore, when a child instinctually plays within their physical world, and the result is a positive experience, then that experience is seen as safe and play will continue. However, if a child encounters a negative experience during their instinctual play, then the result is that of not feeling safe. The child will not continue with that form of play, and, consequentially, will not develop the foundational skills that are typically associated with play. When foundational skills are delayed, so are integration skills, resulting in what is referred to as a *sensory processing disorder.*

Keeping this in mind, a child with a disorganized sensory processing system will seek out play activities that allow them to feel safe. They will also adapt behaviors within the context of their physical world that allow them to feel safe. Since safety is a primary biological need, a child is actually behaving quite normally when they adapt certain behaviors that allow them to feel safe in this physical world that they are trying so desperately to navigate. For example, repetitive behaviors will allow a child to feel safe in their world by giving them a way to control the chaos and providing a sort of grounding. When the world around us seems to be spinning out of control, one way to stop the spinning is to control a small piece of the world and ground ourselves.

With this in mind, it may not be the behavior that we want to change, but rather the experience of how children are connecting within their physical world. This is a very important point not to overlook. If we constantly focus on changing a behavior, which may be a perfectly normal behavior given the child's disorganized sensory processing system, then the result may be that of confusion and frustration for the child, which then can result in more "perceived" negative behaviors. Safety is also important for developing the inner senses, as we will be discussing more in Chapter 9. For now, however, it is important to note that if a child is adapting a behavior that they need in order to feel safe, and we are trying to change the behavior without helping their sensory system to reorganize, then the result can have the child picking up on the sense that there is something wrong with them. That can cause them to shut down even further. Keep in mind that the behaviors a child adopts are in order to provide them with a sense of safety in this confusing world that they are trying to adapt to.

Watching how a child plays can give you clues to what their gifts are. Are they creative, are they more physical, do they tend to be more or less perfectionistic? Are they neat, are they messy and disorganized? Their quirks and their interests are all signs pointing them in the direction of their awesomeness. Watch them in awe, play with them, and enjoy discovering right alongside them. With unbiased eyes, you can watch and discover who your child is, and what their beautiful gifts are. You don't have to mold them, just watch them unfold right in front of your eyes. You can always help strengthen their weaknesses through conditioned play, but don't lose sight of who they are at their core. It is important that you find the balance of helping them with their weaknesses while honoring and celebrating their gifts.

As a therapist, I watch each child with an open mind and with inspiring awe of who they are and what their gifts are. Use their gifts and their strengths as a tool in reaching success within the area of their weaknesses. For example, if a child loves to jump in a ball pit but is not able to climb a ladder, you can encourage and assist them in climbing a ladder so that when they reach the top, they get rewarded by jumping in the ball pit. In the case of Matt, he loved puzzles and loved getting attention from the therapist, so slowly he was able to get used to being tipped backward in order to get a puzzle piece and a silly face from the therapist. Eventually, his vestibular system was able to reorganize itself so that the condition of tipping backward no longer frightened him.

Beyond the Five Senses

Our physical senses connect us with the physical world around us, and there are certainly more than five senses that allow us to do so. In fact, many people have adopted the idea that we have seven or eight main senses, and many scientists have determined that there may be at least 21 physical senses, some of which may be subcategories of a broader sensory system. For example, within the area of taste, we can sense bitter, sweet, salty, sour, and umami (which is the ability to sense the taste of meat). Within the sense of touch, we are able to process separately the senses of pressure, temperature, and itch. Pain is considered separate from touch and can be sensed separately from three distinct types of receptors, which are cutaneous (skin), somatic (bones and joints), and visceral (body organs). Other senses include stretch receptors, chemoreceptors, thirst and hunger receptors, as well as magnetoception and time receptors. We also connect our physical bodies to our physical world through proprioception (a sense of where our different body parts are in relation to other body parts) and equilibrioception (sense of balance and spatial awareness perceived from the vestibular system, which is part of the inner ear). With this sensory system, we can sense movement, including forward and backward, side-to-side, and up and down. This gives us a sense of positional awareness of sitting up, lying on our side or on our back, and being turned upside down.

When a child is born into this physical world, these senses all begin to develop (foundation) and connect (integration), relaying different messages to the brain in response to different experiences. If all is well, then these systems are able to develop strong foundational skills and then integrate with one another in an organized way in order to allow for a natural flow and connection of developmental abilities. This is childhood development in a nutshell. In the case of developmental delays, however, something interferes with this natural process, causing development to stop or alter its natural course. In either case, you have a child that is still connecting with their world but perhaps in a different way than most. Their sensory system is not taking in information from the outside world in an organized manner. Then you add a child's unique personality, family environment, and a number of other factors, and now you can see how there can be so many different possible outcomes. These outcomes are observed and recognized as behaviors.

Behaviors often become labeled as symptoms, and a group of symptoms become categorized as a disorder. In this world that we have created, we often look at things as either normal or abnormal. When development is different from the norm, then it is considered abnormal. In our culture, we tend to want to place a label on anything that appears to be different than the norm. Then we want to "fix" it with therapies and, in some cases, with medication. But what happens when the norms change, when more and more children start reaching their developmental milestones outside the normal range? If more and more children begin perceiving the world differently, norms are bound to undergo statistical change.

As an audiologist, I observed one particular auditory processing test that was revised three times while I was practicing, and each time the norms dropped. Scores that once fell outside the normal range suddenly fell within the normal range statistically based on the new population of children being tested. I often questioned this pattern, wondering if the auditory processing in children was slower to develop due to having so much more visual stimulation. But now I wonder if perhaps something else might be happening. There are so many more senses than just the five that we learned about in school, and it is well-known that when someone loses a sense such as hearing or sight, the other senses become more heightened in order to help that individual connect and navigate around their new sensory processing system. So, what happens when some of these senses become heightened due to human evolution? What if humanity benefits from more and more people being extra sensitive? What if our sensory system is evolving in order to allow for more compassion and more empathy toward each other? What if more and more children are being born with sensitivities that we are yet to discover or accept? What if humanity's survival depends on the evolution of developing and strengthening some of our different or less-used senses?

Key Messages: Unwrapping Senses

» There are more than five senses.

» There are both physical senses and inner senses. Physical senses connect us to and give us information about our physical world. Inner senses connect us to and give us information about our inner world or inner knowing.

» It is important for development that our individual senses connect and integrate with other senses.

» When a child has positive sensory experiences, they will continue to integrate and develop their senses in an organized manner.

» Negative sensory experiences can cause fear and can slow down a child's natural development.

» Positive sensory experiences build physical strength and physical coordination.

» We can change the way the brain processes information by engaging in fun activities that target specific areas of weakness.

» It is important to use play for developing and strengthening the physical senses and equally important to use play for developing and strengthening the inner senses.

» Providing opportunity for both physical and nonphysical play is important for creating balance and harmony within the body.

» Play that is considered to be abnormal play may actually be normal play based on how that individual is processing the world around them.

» Watching a child play can give you clues to where their gifts are.

CHAPTER 2

Unwrapping Language

*Understanding speech and language
development and the common problems that
impact the extra sensitive child*

Speech and language differentiate us from other animals. There are different forms of communication that animals and even plants use to communicate within their species, which can be described as nonphysical, but speech and language is unique to humans. It not only enables us to communicate with one another, but it also allows us to think and reason. Our thoughts and our feelings are nonphysical, and, by developing speech and language skills, we are able to communicate our thoughts and our feelings into physical form. Speech and language in most children develop naturally. What are the essential, foundational skills or building blocks for developing speech and language? In order to simplify this, let's separate the two concepts.

Speech Development

Hearing

First, we will look at speech development. What is essential for the development of speech? The first building block is hearing, but it's not that simple. Normal hearing is important, for when a child is born deaf or with a hearing loss, speech development is often delayed. In fact, in the past, most hearing losses were not diagnosed until a child reached the age of two and their parents noticed that they had not yet started talking. At this point, a child's hearing would be evaluated, and if a hearing loss was present, they would be fitted with hearing aids and begin intensive speech therapy. However, since this child did not have normal hearing and was denied the sense of hearing and the necessary mapping of speech sounds for the first two years of their life, speech development was often very slow to develop, if at all. Today, with early newborn hearing screenings and the use of cochlear implants, children born with a hearing loss have a much better chance of normal speech development than ever before.

Many years ago, I worked with two young girls who were sisters. Mary was born first, and her story matches the typical scenario I just described. She was not talking by the age of two, so the pediatrician recommended a hearing test. It was determined that Mary had severe hearing loss in both ears and was immediately fit with binaural hearing aids. She also began receiving intensive speech therapy. As soon as Mary began to hear for the first time, a whole new world opened up to her. Eventually, Mary began to speak, however, the sound of her voice and her speech had a quality to it very common with hearing impairment. She also had a significant speech and language delay that never quite caught up to what is considered the normal range. About a year after Mary's hearing loss was diagnosed, Annie was born. Since Annie's older sister was diagnosed with a severe hearing loss, Annie's hearing was tested shortly after she was born using the technology that was available at the time, which was reserved for children born at risk for hearing loss. The results were that Annie, too, like her sister, also had a severe hearing loss, and she began wearing hearing aids and receiving intensive speech therapy right away. Annie's speech and language development not only reached typical levels as compared to normal hearing children, they actually surpassed them.

Why do you suppose this occurred? Let's consider the different sensory exposure that each of these sisters experienced. For the first two years of Mary's life, she lived in silence. Normal everyday sounds were not loud enough to stimulate her auditory system, so her brain was not able to create an auditory map in response to sounds. The early foundational skills necessary for speech development comes from our sense of hearing. With early exposure to speech sounds or what can be called sound patterns, the auditory processing system begins to recognize these different patterns of sound and, in turn, begins to put meaning to these different sound patterns. Studies have shown that children by six months of age are already able to recognize the difference between the sound patterns of the language that they are exposed to and of new languages they have not been exposed to. Our brains are pre-wired to learn language in the first few years of our life, and being auditorily engaged with listening is an essential, foundational skill necessary for speech and language development.

Mary's auditory system was not able to engage during the first two years of her life. Her connection with the world around her had to come from her other senses. Communication for Mary had to be developed through her visual system, as well as her sense of what was happening around her. She had to rely on visual cues and environmental factors. Once Mary was fit with hearing aids, she became more auditorily engaged. Sound patterns first became recognizable, then began providing meaning for her so that she could begin communicating verbally with the people around her. However, two years of missing information is very difficult to make up.

Annie, on the other hand, experienced her world very differently than Mary did in the first two years. The hearing aids provided Annie with the hearing necessary to develop sound pattern recognition as a typical-hearing child would. The difference between Annie and a child with typical hearing, however, is that Annie received extra stimulation by participating in speech therapy from the time of her birth. The extra stimulation that Annie experienced provided her with the ability to accelerate her speech and language development to above-average levels.

These two sisters provide us with a unique understanding of the impact of sensory deprivation, particularly hearing loss, upon the development of early speech development. Fortunately, Mary's scenario does not occur very often anymore, especially with the advancement of newborn hearing screenings for all children born in the United States and many other countries. When a hearing loss is present at birth, in most cases it can be diagnosed early, and as demonstrated in Annie's story, early identification is key.

Auditory processing

What happens when at birth the hearing screening shows normal hearing, yet as the child develops they present as if they have a hearing loss? Parents become concerned that their child may not be hearing properly or seems to have "selective" hearing. The hearing tests have shown that the hearing is in the normal range, yet they appear as if they are not hearing much of the time. They may seem to mishear things or get easily confused with directions that have multiple steps. It may appear as if they need extra time to process what they hear, and at times they may even seem to be overly sensitive to sounds or noises. They may cover their ears often in response to certain sounds and may even get quite upset in certain noisy situations. What I am describing here is an auditory processing problem. This can be much harder to diagnose than hearing loss, since the hearing seems to be normal. It can be quite difficult to understand if we think about it in terms of normal hearing, but when we understand the importance of sensory processing development, and particularly auditory processing development, then we can begin to make sense out of this child's particular challenges.

Let's begin with the early stages of auditory processing development. It might surprise you to know that auditory processing development actually begins before birth. Studies have shown that infants are often able to identify their mother's voice among other voices at the time of birth. In fact, the ear begins to hear sounds in the second trimester, and by 24 weeks, babies have been shown to move their heads in response to voices and noises. It is believed that this is what allows babies to begin to acclimate to the physical world through sound vibrations. At birth, they are able to differentiate between voices and different sounds and will often demonstrate what is known as a startle reflex in the presence of a loud or unexpected sound. As with all other sensory processing systems, the auditory system begins connecting the child to the physical world around them, but its function is through sound. As long as hearing is present and the child is auditorily engaged, auditory processing development will usually occur naturally.

Just as a seed innately knows how to grow into a beautiful flower, so does your child intuitively know how to develop processing skills. We are all born with an innate desire to learn, and connecting our human body with the world around us is usually a natural process. As with learning to walk, each step in the process, each foundational skill, is necessary for the next step. As with walking, integration of the different skills is equally important for development to occur.

The important thing to remember is that in order for auditory development to occur, your child must be exposed to sounds and be auditorily engaged with the sounds they are hearing. For example, cooing can begin within the first few weeks and will often continue through three months of age, at which time the gentle cooing of mostly vowel sounds will begin to turn into babbling once the consonant sounds are added. Babbling typically begins around four to six months of age, and by 10 months the babbling may begin to turn into jargon where the individual sounds begin to come together and simulate actual words. It is interesting to note that at this stage of jargon, the sound patterns that a child is putting together relate to the sound patterns of their native language.

This happens as long as the child is auditorily connected and integration is occurring. Think of it this way. Remember from the example of rolling over how the child is intuitively pushing the floor with their arm? Well, with speech, they are instinctively making sounds, and as they are auditorily engaged, they hear the sounds they are making and then realize that as they move their tongue and lips, the sounds that they hear change. They are in control of the sounds. It is through the babbling stage that a child's oral motor skills begin to develop. As long as they are auditorily engaged, they will continue to make different sounds, which leads to the development of oral motor skills. Through repetition, oral motor skills are strengthened, leading to jargon, and eventually to the production of words or speech. When a child is auditorily engaged with their own sound production, vocalizations move from accidental to purposeful, thus resulting in speech development.

As with rolling over, each step in the process is as important as the next one. If early auditory processing skills are not developing normally, the result can cause a child to become auditorily disconnected, resulting in a speech delay. For example, since the cooing and babbling stages begin by accident, if a child does not connect the dots and experience the cause and effect of making different sounds by vocalizing and moving their articulators (i.e., lips and tongue), then the accidental babbling will not become purposeful and will not turn into jargon, the predecessor for meaningful speech. These children are often described as quiet babies and later may be diagnosed as having an oral motor problem or apraxia in severe cases and poor articulation in milder cases. We don't always know what causes auditory processing delays, but there are several possible factors that can place a child at high risk for acquiring a weak or underdeveloped auditory processing system. These factors can include a genetic predisposition, prenatal care or birth trauma, head injury, health or nutritional factors, as well as auditory deprivation.

Auditory deprivation occurs when a child does not receive adequate or consistent auditory input for natural development to occur. Two examples of this, aside from having a diagnosed hearing loss, include chronic ear infections and environments where little care or attention is given to an infant, such as in many orphanages or other environments that may lack adequate stimulation. Within the audiology community, there is much debate regarding auditory processing development and what constitutes a "disorder" and what, if anything, can be done about it. I mentioned many of the possible causes that are usually discussed and accepted as causes, but there is something else that I believe may be contributing to these differences. We may find more answers to these questions when we stop being solely focused on the physical and begin looking beyond the physical. We will be exploring more of what lies beyond our physical senses when we dive deeper into understanding our inner senses.

Common Speech Development Problems

Ear infections and chronic middle ear fluid

A common problem children face today is temporary or fluctuating hearing loss due to excessive fluid in the middle ear. Often, this is diagnosed as an ear infection, but it can also be a problem even if a child does not have a diagnosed ear infection. The result of having a temporary or fluctuating hearing loss due to middle ear dysfunction is a high-risk factor in developing an auditory processing delay or disorder. It is extremely important for the auditory system to hear sounds in order to develop. Sound must travel through the middle ear system in order to reach the inner ear, where it can then send information to the brain and subsequently allow for the development of auditory processing skills. When the middle ear blocks sounds due to fluid or any other blockage, sound reaching the inner ear will be disrupted and information being sent to the brain will not be consistent. In order to develop a good, strong auditory processing system, it is essential that a child hears sounds consistently. When hearing fluctuates, it becomes difficult for the brain to predict and interpret the sound patterns into meaningful words and, later, language. When a child is prone to repeated and prolonged bouts of ear infections or chronic fluid, the effect is often fluctuating hearing loss that can significantly delay auditory processing development. Listening with hearing loss, albeit mild as is often the case, can cause listening to be extra work and can lead to poor listening habits, or selective listening, which can further slow down auditory processing development.

Children are more susceptible to problems with ear infections and middle ear fluid due to the size and shape of their Eustachian tube. With children, the Eustachian tube is shorter and narrower than that of an adult, and it is generally more horizontal than vertical and therefore more prone to blockages. The Eustachian tube connects the middle ear to the back of the throat and, when working properly, allows for air to flow back and forth and provides for proper drainage. When this tube becomes blocked, which can happen during a cold or in response to allergies, fluid can build up in the middle ear space, resulting in hearing loss or fluctuating hearing.

This form of auditory deprivation places a child at risk for auditory processing delays, since auditory processing development relies on a healthy hearing system to transmit sounds to the brain. When sounds are heard consistently, they can be organized and processed into language. When sounds are not heard consistently, listening becomes work, a child becomes a selective listener, and auditory processing development is delayed. When auditory processing development is delayed, listening is more difficult, and poor listening skills often cause difficulties with attention and learning, as well as with social and emotional development.

Low stimulation environment

Just as hearing loss, or even a fluctuating hearing loss, can cause auditory deprivation, so can a low stimulation environment where little care is given to a child. Orphanages are common examples of this type of environment, and I saw many children in my practice who had been adopted from foreign countries where they often received minimal care and little exposure to language. Sometimes, severe health issues, rather than lack of care, can cause a child to be under-stimulated during those critical early developmental stages. For example, a child born prematurely may spend a significant amount of time in a neonatal intensive care unit where they may be exposed to noise levels that exceed what has been accepted as safe by the American Academy of Pediatrics. It has also been suggested that many of these infants are denied adequate exposure to beneficial sounds, such as voices and music.

The first few years of life are critical for learning language. Connecting to people early in development is part of the human experience, and children connect with the people around them through their sensory processing system. Listening to spoken language helps to develop strong auditory processing skills, so when a child is denied this type of human contact, they are more likely to experience a delay in auditory development. Listening is essential to language development, and being exposed to language early on is very important to developing a strong auditory processing system. When children are not exposed to language consistently, delays in auditory development are likely.

In some cases, a child has had adequate exposure to language but that language was different than the language that is spoken in the home after they have been adopted. I observed that often these children who did not have any reported delay in their native language often caught up when exposed to the new language spoken in their new home. However, to ensure that the child does catch up in the new language, I recommend extra auditory stimulation and perhaps a good phonics program to improve the sound pattern recognition more quickly. In cases where a child's native language is not the same language they are learning in school, this can cause a perceived learning challenge. The child experiences a delay in their ability to recognize the sound patterns or the language patterns that they are now expected to use. These children often receive extra help with language but may not receive support for one of the important building blocks of language: auditory decoding or phonemic awareness. Recognizing and strengthening any weakness with auditory decoding or with phonemic awareness can only help with improving listening skills and therefore improving language.

Auditory decoding is not the only auditory processing skill important for language development, but that topic is beyond the scope of this book. However, I do want to acknowledge that auditory processing is a significant and controversial topic. Since this has been a primary area of focus throughout my audiology career, I want to stress the importance of developing a good strong auditory processing system. If you're interested in learning more, there are some great resources, including *When the Brain Can't Hear* by Teri James Bellis, *Auditory Processing Disorders* by Donna Geffner and Deborah Ross-Swain, and the American Speech-Language-Hearing Association (asha.org).

Now, let's dive into the building blocks of language.

Language Development

As speech begins to develop, so does the ability to listen. What a child can say and what they have the ability to listen to tend to develop together. For example, the word "cat" is made up of three different sounds that, when combined together in a sound pattern, become the word we know as cat, a small animal that purrs. At first, a child can only recognize the word cat as one individual sound. The auditory system in the early stages is not fine-tuned enough to recognize the three individual sounds of /c/, /a/, and /t/. But as the auditory system matures, it is able to identify the three individual components of the word cat.

Similarly, a young child can only understand one word at a time then eventually is able to understand and process sentences with two words, then three words, and so on. We often speak to babies and young children with simple one- and two-word sentences, because we recognize that is all their auditory system can handle at that age. As a child gets older, we instinctually expand the number of words we use in a sentence (also called "chunking"). By keeping speech slow and chunking it in the early years, we are able to give the child the appropriate amount of time needed to auditorily process speech and, in turn, learn language. With language that is kept short and simple as well as age appropriate, a child can stay auditorily engaged, thus allowing for listening skills to be acquired and ultimately allowing a good, strong language foundation to develop.

Put another way, in order to develop a good strong language foundation, you must develop good listening skills. In order to develop good listening skills, you must be developing a good, strong auditory processing system. In order to develop a good, strong auditory processing system, you must have a good, strong healthy hearing system and be auditorily engaged. Being auditorily engaged is an instinctual habit. Becoming a good listener is a learned skill. When auditory processing skills are developing naturally, learning to listen can also develop naturally; one helps the other. As long as auditory processing skills continue to develop, listening skills can grow stronger, further allowing for continued auditory processing development, which again, further develops listening skills. Good listening skills are essential to developing a good language foundation.

Selective listening

Being auditorily engaged with the world around us is an instinctual habit that leads to the development of good listening skills as long as the auditory system is developing naturally. Listening to language is extremely important to learning language. A selective listener is only going to learn language when they are listening, so if they are not listening much of the time, then language learning will be delayed. It is very difficult for a part-time listener to develop a good, strong language foundation. Now, let's examine why a child may be a selective listener. Is it just their personality? I do not believe so. It makes sense that in the presence of an auditory processing weakness, listening becomes extra work. And when listening is work, we become selective in what we want to listen to. Think about what it is like listening to someone who is speaking with a very strong foreign accent or dialect. You can listen to the words they are saying, but you have to listen with more effort since your ears do not recognize the sound patterns of their speech as easily as if they were speaking in a more familiar style. This provides a good sense of what it is like for a child who may have an auditory processing weakness, particularly in the area of auditory decoding, which we will discuss further later.

Early auditory development begins by recognizing simple sound patterns spoken clearly and slowly. As your auditory system gets stronger, you begin to recognize those same sound patterns when they are spoken more quickly or in a distorted way, such as when someone has an accent or is simply mumbling. Imagine you are sitting in a waiting room, reading a magazine article. In the first scenario, a couple comes in and sits down beside you and engages in conversation together in your native language. Their conversation may make it difficult for you to concentrate on the article you were reading. Without any effort, you may find yourself listening to and being distracted by their conversation. You may not be trying to listen, but since listening for you is easy and natural, you may have a difficult time ignoring them and concentrating on your reading.

In the second scenario, the couple sitting next to you engages in a conversation in a foreign language that you do not recognize. Now, it is relatively easy to continue reading and concentrating on your article. The conversation taking place next to you is in a language that uses sound patterns that your auditory system does not recognize, so it just becomes meaningless background noise and you are able to block it out. In the third scenario, they are speaking in your native language but with a strong foreign accent. Since their sound patterns are slightly distorted compared to what you are used to hearing, you now have to work hard to listen to them. You can tune them out and read your article if you want to, but if you hear a trigger word that captures your attention, then you have the option to stop reading for a moment and listen to what they have to say. Then if their topic of conversation does not interest you, you can go back to reading, until once again you hear something that captures your attention. Now you have a situation much like the child with an auditory processing weakness in the area of decoding.

This is a good example of selective listening. When listening is work, we tend to selectively choose what we listen to. If it is not interesting to us, then it is quite often not worth the effort it takes to listen. What we put in must equal what we get out, otherwise we may just choose to skip it. Hence, a selective listener is born. In the presence of an auditory processing weakness, delay, or disorder, listening takes extra effort, and therefore it is easily shut down if the information coming in is too difficult or not worth the effort. Because of this, selective listeners are often labeled as having an attention problem or as being easily distracted. Put another way, if their inner senses are more sensitive than what is typical, then they may be paying more attention to their inner talk and therefore present as having an attention problem.

In the above example, the person trying to read the magazine article is distracted by the couple speaking in their own native language. However, when the couple is speaking in a foreign language that has no meaning to that person, then their conversation is quite simply just background noise that they are able to block out. So, what I am suggesting here is that if the information coming in from the *inner senses* is stronger or more interesting than the information coming in from the *physical senses*, then this would cause a person to have difficulty focusing on and connecting with their physical senses.

We will be discussing this further in Part Three; however, for now, let's just consider that an individual who has difficulty staying focused or is easily distracted may have an inner processing system that is louder and more interesting than what is happening in the external. This may present as a possible attention deficit disorder, since that individual is having so much difficulty staying connected to the physical stimuli that is being presented.

Hearing versus listening

Selective listeners often develop a poor language foundation. They may listen to get their needs and wants met, but beyond that, their language development may leave them short when it comes to such things as social skills, understanding the punch line in a joke, abstract thinking and reasoning skills, inference, as well as being overly literal. As a child's language develops, they begin to recognize that words can be used in different ways, such as in idioms and figures of speech. For example, when I told my then two-year-old daughter to jump in the car, she proceeded to get "in" the car and jump. After hitting her head on the roof of the car, she began to cry, and I am sure she was wondering why I had told her to do that. A two-year-old is still processing language very literally. It takes time and repeated listening to begin to understand that words can be used in different ways other than their original meaning.

An important connection to make here is this: just because a child has normal hearing does not mean that they have normal listening skills or normal auditory processing skills. If a child's auditory development is delayed, it is quite possible that, although cognitively they may be growing, auditorily they may not be growing. As a child grows older, we begin to speak to them more quickly and with longer sentences. If a child is chronologically seven years old but has the listening skills of a four-year-old, they may become very confused, insecure, and possibly even angry after unsuccessfully trying to process more advanced language.

I have found that when children are highly intelligent with an auditory processing problem, they typically externalize frustrations with behaviors, because their intelligence level and their performance level don't match. You can imagine how frustrating that might be.

Language and social skills

Another area of auditory processing that we often neglect to recognize is that of intonation, prosody, and melody of speech. Simply processing the sounds of speech and decoding them into a recognizable language is not the only thing to consider when looking at auditory processing. One of the concerns I have heard often from parents is related to their child's ability to pick up on social cues as well as humor and sarcasm in language. For example, ending a sentence as your voice gets higher in pitch usually indicates a question or that you are surprised by the statement. If you end the sentence going down in pitch, it could indicate sarcasm or even melancholy, reminiscent of Eeyore and his pessimistic, gloomy way of speaking. Many children with specific auditory processing difficulties miss these subtleties and therefore can have difficulty in social situations.

Written communication also presents challenges related to auditory processing. Today, we spend more time communicating with one another without verbal language using tools such as email and texting, which allow us to send a message to someone and then wait for a response. One of the problems, however, is that the message may sound different in the receiver's mind than it does in the sender's mind. Intonation, prosody, and melody of speech give us clues to the meaning that the speaker is wanting to convey, and these are lost with written language. For children with auditory processing difficulties, messages are often misinterpreted and can even be mistakenly interpreted as rude, angry, or sarcastic.

Another common concern is that these children often are very literal and have difficulty understanding the double meaning of words. For example, I remember one mom telling me how she and her daughter climbed into the car on a very cold day, and when the mom said, "Ooh, it's warm and toasty in here," her daughter looked at her as if she had two heads and said, "There's no toast in here, Mom." Or, with the example of my daughter hitting her head when I told her to jump in the car, by putting the emphasis on the word "car," then it would mean to get in the car. But if I put the emphasis on the word "in," then it would mean to get in the car and jump. Not picking up on these intonation patterns or the melody and prosody of speech can impact how something is interpreted, which can affect social development and contribute to language processing delays.

Looking at how a child is perceiving the world around them can certainly shed a different light on their behaviors and their challenges. Understanding these perceptual differences is the key to ultimately helping not only our children with developmental delays but every child unwrap their gifts and be comfortable being their true authentic self.

When we don't accept the idea that perceptual differences lead to a different way of connecting and being in the world, then we look for answers based on an outside-in view, which can lead to inappropriate labeling. When we come from the understanding that there is an inside-out explanation for a child's behavior or challenges, then we are that much closer to discovering a true solution. Just focusing on a perceived weakness without truly understanding a child's strengths and honoring those strengths can lead to frustration and feelings of shame, hopelessness, and despair. Our children don't have any trouble learning; we just need to learn to pay more attention to what they are learning instead of what they are being taught.

Key Messages: Unwrapping Language

» Language is what allows us to think and reason as well as communicate our thoughts and our feelings into physical form.

» Thoughts and feelings are nonphysical.

» Normal hearing is not enough for the development of speech and language. Auditory processing is a developmental skill important for speech and language development.

» Listening is important for the development of auditory processing skills, and auditory processing development is important for learning to listen.

» Auditory deprivation is one concern that can delay auditory processing development and can happen in a variety of ways.

» Being auditorily engaged with sounds is important for developing auditory processing skills.

» Oral motor skills develop during the babbling stage.

» Auditory processing development is important for the different stages of speech development, such as cooing, babbling, jargon, speech, and eventually language.

» Not babbling can be a red flag indicating a possible auditory processing delay.

» Chronic ear infections can delay auditory processing development and consequently speech and language development.

» Being a selective listener can be a result of an auditory processing delay and can also further contribute to an auditory processing delay.

» Having extra sensitive inner senses can make it difficult to pay attention.

» Normal hearing does not equal normal listening.

» Understanding how a child is perceiving the world around them is the key to helping them learn and helping them unwrap their gifts.

PART II

*What Are We Really
Teaching Our Children?*

CHAPTER 3

Unwrapping Labels

*Understanding how labels hurt our children
and how inner senses can guide a
paradigm shift*

Language is the bridge we use to learn. The symbols we use to express thoughts, ideas, feelings, and emotions to one another are in most cases words but can also include signs, visual cues, and even music. It is important to realize that language can have many forms and that it is the sharing of information that is of value. Today in our society, we greatly value the ability to learn using verbal language, since that is the primary way in which our schools are set up. It is one of the goals of this book, however, that we come to understand the value of other forms of learning so as to better understand the value of those who learn differently.

Within our present education system, children who have strong language skills, primarily listening and reading, are usually the children with the most success. We are pre-wired to learn language in the first few years of our life. This is typically done naturally by being auditorily connected with our world and learning how to first receive verbal language and then produce and share our verbal language with others. It is fair to then reason that if a child is not auditorily connected with their world, and the outcome is a language delay, that they may then struggle when placed in an environment in which language is the primary bridge for learning.

Does this mean that the child is learning disabled? Yes and no. They are only disabled due to the environment that they are being placed in to learn, but they are not incapable of learning. In fact, when children are placed in the appropriate environment most conducive to their learning style, they will not just learn but will actually thrive in that environment. There are far too many children today who are failing within our education system. This, I believe, is due to so many more children being born today with a different way of processing the world. So far, we have discussed how many of our physical senses connect and develop, and how we can help children develop stronger connections with their physical senses. But if we are going to truly help the children of today, we need to understand how they are evolving and why more and more children are having trouble connecting with the physical world. In order to truly understand this, we must look beyond the physical senses.

Unwrapping the Gift of Inner Senses

French philosopher Pierre Teilhard de Chardin said, "We are not human beings having a spiritual experience. We are spiritual beings having a human experience." Our physical senses are part of that human experience, connecting us to the physical world. However, we are spiritual beings first, and we have senses that connect us to this part of ourselves as well. As the physical senses connect and develop, many of us lose this connection, but what if humanity is evolving in a way that allows us to have the human experience yet still allows us to stay connected to our spiritual side or our divinity? Our inner senses are what keeps us connected to our soul.

What I am suggesting here is that, just as we have more than five physical senses connecting us to the world and allowing us to have the full human experience within our physical body, we also have many different inner senses that keep us connected to our spiritual being, our true essence. We usually refer to these senses as the sixth sense or the sense of intuition, although the range of inner senses is more expansive than this. Just as there are hypo- and hypersensitive physical senses, there are also hypo- and hyper-inner senses. We have some connection to all the different senses, but everyone has their strengths and weaknesses. Some of our senses are just more developed than other senses. In the same way that a natural athlete has strengths related to coordination and agility resulting from a stronger connection with physical senses, such as the proprioceptive, vestibular, and visual integration systems, individuals can have strengths resulting from a stronger connection with their inner senses. We describe children as being visual learners, auditory learners, and multisensory learners, and when it comes to our inner senses, different people have different ways of connecting here as well. We can hear with our inner ears, see with our inner eyes, know with our inner mind, and feel with our inner body. We receive messages and guidance from our inner world through our inner senses, but these inner connections are often replaced with the physical connections that our physical body develops.

A friend of my daughter recently lost his sight due to a car accident and a traumatic brain injury. About 10 months later, we were visiting at my daughter's home and having a conversation about his experience losing his sight and how he was learning to live his life differently. At the time, I was cooking a meal, and he wanted to help me. He explained how he was learning how to cook by sensing things differently, since he could no longer use his physical sight. He proceeded to help me by chopping some of the vegetables and a few other tasks that he could do through touch. He told me how he was noticing a difference with his other senses and how they seemed to be helping him compensate for his lack of sight. In thinking about my friend's experience, I started to wonder if this might help make sense of the experiences of children I had seen in my audiology practice over the years. If children experience an insult to their central nervous system or if genetically they have a weakened ability to develop one or more of their physical senses, then could their inner senses be heightened in order to compensate for their physical weakness?

Now, I am not saying that we don't want to help our children develop strong and healthy connections with their physical senses. What I am suggesting is that more and more children today are coming into this physical world with stronger inner connections, which can be very hard to understand for someone who is not having these experiences. However, it is important that we understand these differences so that we can help our children grow and develop their strengths so that their gifts can be cultivated and shared with the world. Helping them to find balance between the outer senses and the inner senses is the key. For example, if a child who is having difficulty learning verbal language is automatically labeled as language learning delayed, then it is likely that that child will take on the belief that they are not smart enough to go onto college and fulfill their heart's purpose. But what if their intelligence exists in a different form other than verbal language, such as empathy or creativity? Are we serving our children if we label them as deficient in one commonly accepted form of intelligence without searching for their strengths, even if it is in a form that is not typically the focus of schools?

Let's look at Dina's story.

I first saw Dina when she was in the eighth grade. Mom had made the decision to pull Dina out of the public school system at the end of the seventh grade and homeschool her. Dina was very sensitive and had been very overwhelmed on a daily basis in middle school. She started shutting down more and more, her self-esteem started to really suffer, and she was significantly behind in reading, which contributed to her overwhelm and self-doubt. She did not like going to school, and it was causing her a lot of anxiety. Dina spent her eighth grade learning at home and working with me to address her auditory processing weaknesses and, consequently, her reading challenges. We also worked on improving her sensory integration. By the end of that year, she had made remarkable improvement both in her reading and her overall self-esteem, and she enrolled in public high school where she was successful both academically and socially. She went on to attend university, where she received her four-year degree and then attended nursing school where she specialized in pediatric oncology. I had always been struck by Dina's kind nature and her empathy toward others, and her compassionate qualities guided her into a profession where those traits are essential. Yes, school was often challenging for her, but she had purpose and a strong desire to make a difference in the lives of children and their families. If she had not had the experience of success that year in which she was homeschooled and instead continued to feel as if she was not smart enough, then perhaps her gifts would have remained hidden. In the end, Dina's gifts were unwrapped, and today she is providing a beautiful and much-needed service to many children and families facing significant health challenges.

What I am proposing is that there are other forms of intelligence than what we traditionally measure in our schools today. There is an inner intelligence that we are neglecting to see, because we are so focused on the outer development. Creativity, imagination, problem-solving, and empathy are all important forms of knowledge that we can be helping our children to cultivate. When we begin to understand this, then we will begin to see the potential that every child has to learn. It's just that learning may look a little different than it has in the past. We have been conditioned to discount and ignore inner intelligence and have narrowed our focus to helping our children develop external intelligence. What I am proposing here is that we observe our children, help them identify their strengths, and honor their strengths, no matter where those strengths are coming from. This way, we can have more Dinas in the world sharing their gifts.

Inside of every child are beautiful gifts just waiting to be unwrapped. It's time we change the lens of our mind through which we are looking at our children and start looking at them through the lens of our heart. As Wayne Dyer has said, "If you change the way you look at things, the things you look at change." We have all been conditioned to see the world through what society and our culture has shown us in the past, but the old paradigm is no longer serving our children of today. It is time for a paradigm shift.

Looking Beyond Limiting Labels

In our culture, it is common to want to place labels on our children. We study our children statistically and measure their development. When a behavior or particular developmental skill falls outside of what is considered typical or normal development, then we feel the need to label it. We use labels such as ADHD, dyslexic, and autistic to describe a set of behaviors that are typical within each of the label's scope. Our development and the way we behave in our environment is therefore observed and then labeled based on whether or not it falls within the normal range. If it falls outside of what is considered the normal range, then a label is placed on that child. However, a child's development is relative to the way they are perceiving the world through their senses, and if there are delays or differences, then we want to identify which sensory areas are delayed or disorganized in the way they are perceiving and integrating the information rather than apply a catch-all label to the child.

I often use the term *neurological disorganization* as a description of what is happening with each child I see in my practice and then try to pinpoint which sensory areas that are in need of improved organization. Labels such as ADHD, dyslexia, and autism, just to name a few, are all used to describe behaviors associated with disorganization or delays in particular sensory areas. The problem here is when there is overlap and there are multiple labels being used, which often happens due to the nature of our sensory processing system. For example, I have had parents tell me that their child's difficulty hearing in background noise is due to their ADD and not due to an auditory processing problem. Because they have fully committed to the label, they look for medication to solve the problem without acknowledging the potential positive impact of strengthening the organization of the auditory system. I have also been told by educators that I was wasting my time trying to improve a child's auditory processing abilities, because the child has autism and that's just part of being autistic. When we look at labels this way, we can easily do harm to a child by not recognizing their true abilities and potential.

By recognizing the uniqueness of each child's neurological system and pinpointing their strengths and weaknesses, we are able to put together a plan that will help them develop and integrate their sensory weaknesses while balancing and harmonizing the whole child. At the same time, we want to pay attention to a child's inner senses in order to help them balance and integrate those abilities as well. I see children and their particular development as what is unique to them through their unique processing system. In Part One, we explored how a child connects to their physical world through their physical senses. These different sensory areas allow them to interact with their environment, and their sensory system is unique. The inner senses, however, are often overlooked, yet they play an important role in a child's development as well. Not every sensitive child is going to present the same way. In fact, I believe that we are all sensitive on some level, or at least we start out that way, but some of us maintain a greater inner sensitivity as we develop than others.

Since our culture is so used to labeling behaviors, sensitive children have also fallen prey to labeling. Labels such as HSC or Highly Sensitive Children, Empaths, Crystal Children, and Indigo Children are all labels that have been used to describe varying levels of sensitivities that different children possess. Using these labels can be helpful in understanding a child's differences, however, it can also be confusing when you are trying to see where a child falls on the spectrum of sensitivity. What I propose is that we simply look at sensitivity as the way that different individuals are perceiving the world through their inner senses, and by observing their strengths and weaknesses we can help to identify a child's particular gifts in order to help guide them on their path. By honoring the gifts and strengths that each child possesses, both with their inner senses and with their physical senses, we can honor who they are and help them to discover their authenticity and their purpose. That does not mean we get rid of labels altogether. Rather, we should look at the whole child and label their strengths first. This will help children to identify with their awesomeness and therefore cultivate a positive sense of self.

Temple Grandin's story is an illuminating example of how gifts associated with higher sensitivity threaten to be buried underneath labels attached to behavior. In her early years, Temple was diagnosed with special needs and later diagnosed with autism in her teens. She struggled with repetitive speech, tantrums, and anxiety and was often teased by her peers. Beneath the labels, she possessed a gift for sensitivity, which eventually led to an invention often used in sensory integration therapy clinics.

Temple's gifts included an extremely high intelligence, especially in the area of science and an extraordinary way of connecting with animals. As with many individuals with autism, Temple had difficulty relating with people and spent a lot of time alone. A common observation of individuals with autism is that they have a difficult time connecting with anything from outside of themselves. Specifically, they have difficulty connecting and organizing the outside world through their physical senses. With that in mind, they are often more comfortable withdrawing from the physical world and can be described as going deep within themselves.

As a young girl, Temple noticed that the cattle at her aunt's ranch appeared to be calmed by the squeeze chutes that cattle "squeezed" into while they were being examined. Realizing this, Temple placed herself in the chute and found the gentle squeezing of the machine reduced her stress and anxiety. She later went on to develop the squeeze machine, or "hug machine," to reduce her own anxiety and overstimulation. However, she was ridiculed for her odd behavior and was forced to use her squeeze machine in secret. With the encouragement of her science teacher, she continued to refine the hug machine's development and explore why it worked. Now, it is a tool that many sensory integration therapists use in their clinics to help individuals who struggle with anxiety from overstimulation.

Another observation that Temple made, and one that upset her quite a bit, was how the cattle were treated on their way to slaughter. Cruelty in the way these animals were treated impacted her in a monumental way. Her empathy toward the animals caused her to feel what they were feeling. She was able to feel their fear and their pain. In an effort to help them, she designed a more humane way of guiding and treating the cattle that would greatly reduce their fear and pain. Due to her natural gift with mathematics, she was able to see and design these systems in her mind and estimate the cost of the project down to the penny. This is how she was able to outbid her competitors and begin her business, which up until this time had been a male-dominated endeavor. Temple Grandin later went on to form her company, Grandin Livestock Handling Systems, Inc., which is still in operation today.

The story of Temple Grandin is a remarkable example of how an individual's gifts, once perceived as disorders, when understood and developed can change the world. Her sensitivity towards animals and her ability to understand and translate those emotions into a therapeutic device has helped many children and families. As well, her empathy towards animals and her mathematical genius have transformed the livestock industry and have forever changed the way animals are treated.

As time goes on, I believe we will start to identify a child's gifts by how they may be perceiving not only their physical world but also their inner world. In Dr. Judith Orloff's book *The Empath's Survival Guide: Life Strategies for Sensitive People*, she discusses the difference between highly sensitive people and empaths. While highly sensitive people are able to accurately identify others' feelings, empaths actually take on the emotions of others. They may be able to feel others' pain as if it were their own and may have difficulty distinguishing which feelings are theirs and which feelings belong to someone else. Some empaths are capable of having profound spiritual and intuitive experiences. Dr. Orloff describes what she calls the *empathic spectrum*, with empaths on the far right and empath-deficient individuals on the far left (e.g., narcissistic, sociopathic, or psychopathic). In between the two extremes, loving empathic people fall in the middle and highly sensitive people fall close to empaths.

When we develop and focus more on our inner senses, then we are more likely to look deep within ourselves for the answers. This inner knowing is where true strength lies. This is what will create a paradigm shift. I believe this is what is happening today, and more and more children are being born more sensitive in order to support this change. We are seeing a strong and steady shift to the right of the spectrum, where more caring people are becoming more sensitive, more sensitive people are becoming more highly sensitive, and more highly sensitive people are becoming more empathic.

A question I would like to pose here is this: can a sensitive child move further left on the spectrum if their natural sensitivities are not cultivated and nurtured? In Chapter 9, we will look at how trauma can affect a sensitive child on a deeper level and how a child can move from one side of the spectrum to the other side as a result of their environment.

In order to support this paradigm shift, we need more sensitive children, and that is exactly what we are experiencing. But these children need our help. Sensitive children can come in many different packages and receive many different labels such as Autism Spectrum, Asperger's, Down's Syndrome, ADD, ADHD, Dyslexia, Learning Disabled, Language Delayed, Shy, and Typical Developing. But the one thing they all have in common is that they have a stronger connection with their inner senses, and it is up to us to help them grow and develop these beautiful gifts. This is the evolutionary leap that we are seeing today. Finding balance and harmony with all our senses, I believe, is the key to helping our children today. In my practice, I found that as time went on, I began seeing more and more children who were diagnosed with sensory integration dysfunction or sensory processing disorder also show signs of being extremely sensitive or even empathic and have heard from parents, teachers, and therapists who have also observed this trend. When we stop focusing on what we label as wrong, we may actually see the beautiful gift.

Key Messages: Unwrapping Labels

» It is important to shed light on the different ways children learn and to begin to value these differences.

» A child may be learning-disabled due to the environment they are in if their learning style is not honored and developed.

» Labels can limit a child's ability to succeed and develop their true gifts.

» Labeling a child's strengths can support developing a positive sense of self and unwrapping their true potential.

» Temple Grandin's story is a good example of how unwrapping an individual's gifts can greatly affect the world in a positive way.

» All children are born sensitive; however, life experiences can nurture and cultivate, or traumatize and shut down.

» Sensitivity is an attribute that all children possess, but there are different levels and different gifts that are unique to everyone.

» Parents, teachers, and other professionals have been reporting that they are seeing more and more sensitive children today.

CHAPTER 4

Unwrapping Belief Systems

Understanding how the highly sensitive child
learns self-limiting beliefs and a new model to
teach self-love

My brother grew up with an undiagnosed learning disability. As an adult, he was eventually diagnosed as having Auditory Processing Disorder and ADHD. As a child, he struggled in all areas of his life, at home, at school, and with friends. He was described as a smart kid, but he didn't pay attention or listen, and was viewed as not working hard enough. The school suggested that he repeat first grade, and so he did, but he still struggled to keep up with his peers. The school thought he had trouble learning, but the truth is he did not have any trouble learning at all. He learned that he was not as smart as the other kids and that no matter how hard he worked, he would still come up short. He learned failure. There was not a lot known about learning disabilities such as APD and ADHD back then, and therefore he did not receive any support. He was left struggling with the blame being put on him for not applying himself, and the fact that our parents were separated meant that not having a father at home must be the cause. With my mom being a single parent during a time when this was not very common or accepted, there was a lot of pressure on her to work and support us. This created even more difficulty when she would be called at work and told that she had to pick up her son, because he was misbehaving again in school.

Since there was little to no understanding about what was going on inside of my brother and everything was being blamed on external circumstances, my brother was left feeling stupid and smart at the same time. His inner knowing was trying to convince him of his genius and was trying to guide him, but external circumstances continued to shout at him that he was a failure. This is certainly a lot for a young mind to have to sort through. There was no support for him at school, and he did not feel supported at home either. So, his worldview had to be created in a way that would not cause him pain. He had to create beliefs that would support him internally, since he was not feeling supported at all from external sources. He had to develop beliefs such as the world is not fair, people are stupid, people with book smarts have no common sense, and no one gets me. His worldview has followed him throughout his life and has caused him a lot of pain, anger, and helplessness. This is how a beautiful, sensitive child full of love, joy, and humor adapts and changes in order to protect themselves from the pain of self-limiting beliefs.

You see, my brother was actually very smart, and still is. He just grew up during a time when his differences were rare and not understood. Back then, there was little being taught about different learning styles, and everyone was expected to learn the same material in the same way. My brother was not broken, and he did not have to be fixed or changed. What he needed was love, understanding, and support. He needed to have experiences where he was able to feel good about his gifts, where he could experience success instead of constant failure, and where he would know that it was not only okay to be who he is but also that he is an extraordinary presence in this world.

Today, there are many more children like my brother, and we are making progress in helping them. However, what usually happens is we label them, then with medication, therapy, and other services, we try to make them fit into the system we have in place, which creates negative beliefs when the child doesn't fit into that system. A life lived with negative beliefs is like serving prison time for a crime you did not commit. As parents, we often think a lot about keeping our children healthy by being careful about what we put into their bodies in the form of food. But what about the things we are feeding their minds? We are feeding them our beliefs from our own experiences in a world based on an old paradigm. As teachers and therapists, we are so focused on helping these children "fit in" and succeed that we can easily do more damage by continuing to program into their minds that they are broken and that they need to be fixed in some way. When a child is in constant need of extra services, no matter how much progress they are making, they eventually take on the belief that they are forever flawed.

I am reminded of one particular child I worked with years ago who taught me more than I taught him. When I started working with Jay, I would have to spend the beginning of each session trying to persuade him to come out from under the couch in the waiting room. We even spent several therapy sessions working under the therapy table. Eventually we bonded, and he was for the most part pretty cooperative, but his delays were so significant that even the simplest of tasks were often too difficult for him. I had to break the steps down further than I had ever had to do in the past, since his noncompliant behavior was a direct reflection of how difficult the task was. It was frustrating to watch him refuse to try a task when I knew he could do it. Jay's refusal to even try was one of the biggest complaints that I heard from his parents and from his teachers. It was also frustrating for me as well, until I realized that here was a kid who had spent all day in school where no matter how hard he tried, he could not experience success and then he had to come to my office immediately after school with no down time and, yet again, be faced with tasks that he struggled with. Jay's strategy of dealing with his own inner feelings of shame for not being good enough caused him to make the only choice he felt he could make. He made a conscious choice to shut down and stop trying. He adopted this behavior in order to protect himself from his deep feelings that he could no longer bear to feel.

However, once the task was broken down into steps that he could successfully complete, he started working harder. I will never forget the first time he had a breakthrough. I can't even express the joy on his face when he first completed a task that he had been struggling with from the start and had all but given up on ever accomplishing. But once I figured out that his auditory processing system was so significantly delayed that even the simplest of tasks were challenging to him, then I was able to break down the task even further until he was able to succeed. It is also important to note here that Jay was extremely sensitive and caring with a tremendous affection toward animals. However, his repeated experiences of failure left him feeling devalued and, at times, hopeless that he could ever succeed at anything. I am not sure how Jay is doing today, but I certainly hope that if it hasn't happened yet, that someday his beautiful gifts will be unwrapped.

Today's children hold the key to the future of humanity, and this key lives in the heart of every child. Like Jay and my brother, their hearts are huge, and because they feel so deeply, they break easily. I truly believe that it is time that we reconnect with our own divinity by helping our children experience theirs. Honoring who they are, opening communication for them to feel safe with their own emotions, and helping them feel good about who they are is a good place to start. Now this may sound like an enormous task, but it is a natural way of being for each of us. Yes, we may have to unlearn what our experiences have taught us, but the good news is that it is our true nature. It is just a matter of remembering who we are and connecting with our children's hearts that will help us remember ours.

New Computer, New Opportunity

I recently purchased a new computer. Of course, one of the first things that they do with a new computer is to start transferring everything from the old computer to the new computer. This time, I was surprised to see that, with the click of a button, everything from my old computer magically appeared onto my new computer. I remember thinking, "Wait! Stop!" I don't want everything from my old computer on my new computer. I have a lot of junk and old files that I don't want cluttering up my new computer. Part of me really wanted to start fresh, clean, uncluttered, but do I really want to start all over and take on all of that myself? Starting from scratch can be scary, and maybe it is best just to transfer everything over to the new computer since then I don't have to worry about not having something that I may need one day. After all, this new computer has more memory, so I should be fine for a while, right? Well, at least until it is time to buy another new computer. Then I had the task of learning new ways of doing things, and for a couple of weeks, my new computer actually sat on the side of my desk as I reached for my old computer. Eventually, I had to take the time to learn all the new features and new ways of doing things, and over time I have learned to love my new computer and all the things I can do now that I could not do before. Now with a push of a key, I can easily erase the old programming from before and only use the new programming.

Wouldn't it be nice if we could change our own internal programming with the swipe of a key, like a new computer? Most of us, if we really take the time and look at ourselves, will find that there are plenty of things we would love to change. And the truth is that we have the power to do just that. With all of today's neuroscience research, we know this can be done. In the book *Breaking the Habit of Being Yourself: How to Lose Your Mind and Create a New One*, Dr. Joe Dispenza discusses the scientific reasons behind how we acquire self-limiting beliefs and how society plays a role in our own self-concept. He uses sciences such as quantum physics, neuroscience, biology, and genetics to demonstrate how we can reprogram them through meditation and other mindfulness techniques. He does a beautiful job bridging science with spirituality. By understanding how our own self-limiting beliefs are created, we can see how a child who is constantly experiencing failure would create their own worldview in order to ease their pain of feeling inadequate. We can also see how a child who is hypersensitive to their environment would feel the need to create a world that would help them to feel safe.

Our life is constantly sending us messages that are meant to help us reprogram ourselves. These messages usually come in the form of discomfort. When we are feeling overwhelmed, angry, anxious, or other negative emotions, it is usually a sign that the thoughts we are having at that moment are not leading us in the right direction. It is our internal GPS that is trying to redirect us. Inside of each of us is an inner knowing of who we really are. Unfortunately, we are guided down paths in all different directions based on belief systems that we have had programed into us and that we have programmed into ourselves based on our own experiences. Knowing what I know now about my computer, I am being very careful about what I program into it, because I don't want it to get cluttered up with a bunch of junk again. Based on my previous experiences with my past computers, I feel as if I will be able to do a better job with this new one. The more we know about the programs we are putting into our computer and how our computer works, the better choices we can make. By paying more attention to what goes in from the start, I know I will have a much more efficient processing system over time.

Using this idea, we can gain a better understanding of the experiences of children today and how to best support them; they are updated humans who are being programmed with outdated belief systems. There are far too many beautiful sensitive children suffering today, because we don't understand them. They have beautiful gifts that are going unrecognized and covered up, because we are so focused on the external that we fail to recognize the beauty that lies within. Since we do not recognize it, it is hard for the child to recognize it, and therefore false, self-limiting beliefs begin to form. But what if we can begin downloading upgraded programming right from the start? Our children are coming into this world with this new and beautiful operating system, and it is time we stop programing the old beliefs and begin matching their upgraded operating system with new and improved programming so there will be less need for them to work extra hard later to erase and reprogram. We all know how hard it is to change our internal programing system after years of operating from our limiting beliefs. Yes, it is possible, and billions of dollars are spent each year on programs and therapists designed and trained to help us change that programing. We can continue to download our old outdated programming into them with our limiting beliefs and old societal paradigm, or we can make a conscious effort to learn all we can about this new way of processing information so that we can begin downloading experiences that will better support this new and improved operating system. The more we understand about how the brain learns, how the body develops, and how our moods and personalities are molded, the better equipped we are to help our children with their own programming.

Every child is a treasure just waiting to be discovered. Unfortunately, all too often we are so busy running around trying to mold and shape them that we don't realize they are already perfect. We spend so much time comparing them to an old societal paradigm that we miss the beauty of who they truly are. Too many beautiful children are being lost, because they are not understood. They are being put into environments that are not conducive to the way they learn and the way they are perceiving the world. We misunderstand their behaviors, and because they are perceiving the world differently, we want to categorize their behaviors, label them, and then treat them. More and more children everyday are being diagnosed with various learning or developmental differences. People are searching for answers, treatments, and cures, but what if the answer is right in front of our noses? What if the simple answer is to stop trying to make a square peg fit into a round hole? What if we just readjust the hole so that all the differently shaped pegs could fit in easily? Now, this does not mean that we do not help our children. It just means that the help we need to give them may look a little different than it has in the past. We need to first take a good look at how they are processing differently and then work to understand why they may be processing differently. When a child processes the world around them differently, then their experiences will be different. Since our experiences play such a dominant role in how we form our beliefs about ourselves and the world, then understanding and accepting these differences is the first step in truly helping our children.

Giving a Child the Gift of New Beliefs

Leah never had any difficulty learning. She always did well in school and could even be described as an overachiever. Even though she earned good grades, she often would not feel as if they were good enough. She put a lot of pressure on herself to be what she considered perfect. Leah was very sensitive, and with her sensitivity she was very compassionate toward others and felt a strong desire to make sure those around her were happy. She felt as if it was her job to make sure that the people around her were cared for and nurtured. Leah loved stuffed animals and made sure that all of her stuffed animals had names and that they all had turns spending time with her. When asked if she had a favorite, she said no because she loved them all equally and would not want to hurt any of their feelings. Leah was very sensitive to the feelings of other people and did not like being exposed to conflict or negativity. She always felt the need to stick up for the underdog and would neglect her own needs in order to be caring and compassionate toward others. As she grew up, she continued to put herself last. Leah never felt good enough and was more comfortable being alone than being in large groups. By the time she was in high school, she was being treated for anxiety disorder and a fear of failure. Leah's world was confusing due to all the different emotions that she was feeling. She would not only feel what other people were feeling, but she would also take those feelings on as her own, which made it very difficult for her emotionally. She was often told that she was too sensitive, and so she grew up feeling as if she had to hide that part of herself. The worldview that she adopted as her own was one in which being sensitive was a weakness that needed to be kept hidden. Leah never felt safe being her own authentic self, so she found it easier to stay quiet.

Every child is born into this world with beautiful gifts that they are meant to share with the world. However, as is so often the case, these children are placed in situations in which they are not successful or not good enough, and therefore they begin developing a narrative that they are not successful and not good enough. This story often follows these children throughout their childhood and into their adult lives. Many of us do find our way eventually, often with therapy and self-help books, but how about those who don't overcome their early story? What about those who make choices based on this story and end up in repeated patterns of self-doubt, fear of failure, lack of worthiness, and feelings of stupidity. In our society, these are often the individuals who end up on unemployment and, in more severe circumstances, juvenile detention centers and even prison. These are the individuals who often find relief by self-medicating and find themselves with negative addictions, full of anger and hopelessness.

I can go on and on with the negative side effects of this problem, but what I prefer to do is explore the "what if?"

- What if every child was able to see themselves for the beautiful soul that they are?

- What if every child could go to school and come home feeling successful, eager to share what they have learned with their parents?

- What if every child had the opportunity to develop their beautiful gifts and share them with the world?

- What if every child could be seen in their own uniqueness with a sense of awe?

- What if a child who could build a city out of Legos was seen as gifted in the same way as a child who can read and understand a book is seen as smart?

- What if all children could come together in a place and honor each other for their own unique genius, whatever it may be?

- What if a child who can communicate beauty through their genius of art was able to feel as smart and valuable as a child who understands science?

- What if a child who could listen to a piece of music once and play it back with every ounce of their soul's passion was seen as important as the child who excels in math?

- What if the child who could take things apart and put them back together was praised for their abilities?

- What if a child who was physically strong and agile on the playground was able to value their gifts and express them in a positive and meaningful way that would assist others?

- What if every child was able to value their unique gifts as equal in importance as all others?

- What if every child woke up in the morning eager to go to school and learn something new?

- What if we could all live in a world of non-judgement and value each and every one of us as the genius that we are?

What if........what if.......what if........

Take a moment and fill in the blank here. What treasured gifts can you see our beautiful, unique children sharing with the world? Within every child is a beautiful soul here on earth to share their gifts. To quote one of my favorite songs:

Don't know much about history
Don't know much biology
Don't know much about a science book
Don't know much about the French I took
But I do know that I love you
And I know that if you love me, too
What a wonderful world this would be

All any of us wants is to be loved, by ourselves and others. When we grow up not feeling valued, it can be very difficult to love ourselves, which in turn can make it very difficult to allow others to love us. When a child is placed in an environment in which they cannot be met with success, then feeling successful is extremely difficult. Repeatedly experiencing situations in which they are not successful or deemed unworthy can lead to low self-esteem and lack of value. Feelings of lack of value can leave a child feeling unlovable, even into adulthood. Even if a child grows up in an extremely loving home, feelings of low self-esteem and unworthiness can lead to lack of self-love.

Love is our true nature. We all come from love, of love, by love, for love. When we allow ourselves to be cut off from love, we can spend our entire lives searching for it only to eventually find that it has been within us the entire time. Authenticity is the key. If we can allow and encourage our children to remain connected to their heart and their true nature, they will find that their truest sense of self is love, and we can all learn to love the genius within each and every one of us.

Key Messages: Unwrapping Belief Systems

» Children need to have experiences of success in order to feel successful.

» Children create a worldview based on their own experiences as well as the beliefs that are passed along within the family and society.

» The more we discover about how the brain learns, the body develops, and personalities get molded, the better equipped we are to help our children develop their own positive self-concept.

» Helping our children today looks different than it has in the past.

» Our experiences shape the way we see ourselves and the way we see the world around us.

» Every child is born into the world with beautiful gifts that are meant to be shared with the world.

» Feelings of unworthiness and of being unlovable come from repeated experiences that foster these feelings.

» Authenticity is the key to self-love and a positive sense of self.

CHAPTER 5

Unwrapping Society

Understanding the old and new paradigms
and their implications for the highly sensitive
child

Today, we hear more and more stories about people reaching enormous success who at one time or another were considered "misfits" or were the target of physical and emotional bullying. Many of these now-famous people are opening up about these painful secrets in their pasts. Successful celebrities like Ed Sheeran, Lady Gaga, and Sia have recently appeared in Goalcast's video series to share how they were teased and made fun of during their childhood for being overly shy and awkward. Many great leaders, pioneers, and artists who have shared similar struggles include: Bill Gates, Steve Jobs, Susan Boyle, Tim Burton, Charles Darwin, Emily Dickenson, Nikola Tesla, Jerry Seinfeld, Sir Isaac Newton, Michelangelo, Mozart, Thomas Jefferson, Daryl Hannah, Dan Aykroyd, and Henry Cavendish.

It is easy to see that individuals who have been considered neurodiverse, or simply different, have impacted this world in so many ways. Looking at these people and all they have contributed shines a light on the truth that each of us at our core is our own genius. It reinforces the idea that success does not have to look a certain way and that it can come in all sorts of packaging. It is not important what the wrapping looks like. What is important is seeing the beauty on the inside. Many of our children today are hiding behind their unique wrapping, afraid of being seen or heard due to their perceived differences. Helping our children feel safe and valued is not only a gift for them but is also ultimately a gift for society and humanity. Within a society based on cooperation instead of competition, more children will grow up comfortable with expressing themselves and with their own authenticity.

The Heart of a Sensitive Child

As we discussed earlier in Part One, we know how important it is for our physical senses to organize and develop a good, strong connection with our physical world. We also talked a little bit about our inner senses and how we don't typically put very much emphasis on helping children develop these senses. In fact, as the physical senses grow stronger, our inner senses often become weaker. The old saying "if you don't use, you lose it" can certainly apply here. Children who have diagnosed developmental delays have physical senses that are not developing at the same time or rate that is statistically within the normal range based on collected data; however, their inner senses may be quite heightened or advanced compared to typical children. This does not mean, though, that only children with disorganized sensory processing systems will develop strong inner senses. Today, more and more children are being born extra sensitive. They may or may not have extra sensitive physical senses, but their inner senses start developing at a heightened level early on. The fact that many children today can be described as being highly sensitive presents real challenge at times, since these children may not show any signs of having a delay, yet being highly sensitive can have a tremendous impact on the way they learn and interact with others.

In the books *The Highly Sensitive Person* and *The Highly Sensitive Child,* Elaine Aron describes the challenges that highly sensitive people face in this world. She uses the acronym DOES to describe the four main attributes of a highly sensitive person.

- *Depth*. They process information more deeply. They tend to reflect and be deep in thought.

- *Overstimulation*. They can become easily overstimulated.

- *Empathy.* They feel very strong emotions and empathy toward others.

- *Sensitivity.* They are far more sensitive to subtleties.

For me, growing up highly sensitive was a tremendous challenge. I did not struggle in school academically, but I did struggle socially. I never felt as if I fit in anywhere. I often thought it was because we moved quite often; I never went to the same school or school district for more than three years. Between first grade and my senior year in high school, I moved six times and attended seven different schools in New York, Georgia, and Texas. Now, that would be challenging for anyone, but for a highly sensitive child, that had its own set of challenges. I was always being told that I was too sensitive, and therefore I felt as if this was a huge flaw. I saw it as a weakness, and I was always trying to hide it. I was often embarrassed by my inability to hold back my tears and was often picked on and made fun of. I was an easy target for bullying, since I would not fight back. I never seemed to get angry and mostly felt hurt.

Only recently, I have come to realize that what I perceived as my weakness as a child was actually my superpower. As an audiologist, I have been able to convey a deep empathy toward my patients who are able to feel and trust, knowing that I truly have their best interest in mind. When I consult with parents about their children, they often remark on how I am able to know so much about their child after just one session. To me, it always seemed like common sense, but I now know that I have an inner knowing of things that are not as apparent to others as they are to me. Looking back now on my childhood, I can see clearly how my sensitivity affected me in so many ways. I felt that this beautiful gift was an awful curse, and I just wanted to keep it hidden. In doing so, I also kept my true essence hidden. I played different roles, always trying to be the person I thought others wanted me to be. I often put myself last and would do for others first, hoping to be liked.

When children grow up not feeling comfortable with who they are, they have to work hard at trying to be someone they are not. This is certainly not a recipe for success. Being sensitive is not a curse, but a gift and a blessing. I truly believe more and more children are being born extra sensitive today, because it is what our world needs. However, it is very important that these children be understood and seen for the beautiful souls that they are. It is imperative that these children develop their gifts, are proud of their gifts, and are not afraid to be seen with their gifts. What good is a gift if it remains hidden without being shared? It is time that we help our children grow and develop their gifts so that they can be shared with the world. Understand that sensitivity is not a weakness, but rather it is a beautiful strength. Sensitivity is an upgrade. Here are some examples of the gifts sensitive children tend to possess:

- *Creativity.* Highly sensitive children tend to be very creative and think outside the box. They are our artists, our musicians, our inventors. Allow these qualities to grow and develop. These are skills to be proud of.

- *Empathy.* Highly sensitive children are empathic toward others. They are our humanitarians, and they make good leaders. Some famous people who are considered to have been highly sensitive include Abraham Lincoln, Eleanor Roosevelt, Martin Luther King Jr., Albert Einstein, and Mother Teresa, just to name a few.

- *Depth of thought and emotion.* They feel more deeply and think more deeply. Highly sensitive children feel things more intensely. They often show kindness and empathy toward others and may need some guidance in how best to support others without putting themselves last.

- *Keen observation.* Highly sensitive children are often described as shy or introverted. This is often seen as a negative, but consider instead that they are actually strong observers of social interaction. By observing rather than participating, they are able to discover and reflect on a deeper level what is going on around them. This provides insights into human nature and helps them develop a strong inner knowing.

- *Connection to nature.* They are often attracted to nature. Being in nature is very calming for them. Often, they are drawn towards animals and may choose professions that allow them to connect and work with animals.

Building Self-Esteem

One of the biggest concerns I have heard from parents throughout the years was their concern about their child's self-esteem. Children who are extra sensitive will often have a harder time developing a good strong self-esteem. Building a strong self-esteem comes from four main areas. The first is from your immediate family. Knowing that you are truly loved and accepted for who you are is important for developing a strong sense of self in this area. As we have mentioned before, sensitive children will often feel things much deeper. If they do not feel accepted within their own family dynamics for who they are, then feelings of not being good enough or as good as a sibling are likely to have a greater impact. Everyone's family dynamic is unique, but it is important that you look at the way a child might be seeing the situation.

For example, if a sensitive child has a sibling with special needs, then it is likely that a lot of attention is being devoted to that sibling. The child who is sensitive may interpret this as if they are not as important as the other child. They may act out and try to gain attention, or they could just withdraw and try extra hard to be perfect hoping that will get their parents' attention. Every child has special needs, it's just that every child's needs are different. Try and look at things through the child's eyes in order to see what they may be seeing and feeling. It is very important, especially for a sensitive child, to feel that they are loved and valued within the dynamics of their family.

The next important place where we develop our self-esteem is in social situations. As a child develops their language skills and begins interacting socially with those around them, they begin to see how they provide value within their relationships. They develop their sense of worth by how others like them and interact with them. Because sensitive children feel things deeper and often feel what other people are feeling around them, they may become easily overwhelmed in certain social situations, especially situations consisting of large groups. Oftentimes sensitive children will prefer smaller groups and more one-on-one interactions. Allowing them opportunities for successful interactions with others is important. If small groups or one-on-one situations work best, then it is a good idea to provide ample opportunity for those types of interactions. Pushing them to socialize in large groups when they are not comfortable in those environments can cause the sensitive child to internalize even more deeply how they just don't fit in.

Next, we have physical self-esteem. This is where a child needs to feel safe and comfortable in their body. This can be difficult for a sensitive child if they are having challenges with their physical senses. However, it is not about being the athlete or the ballerina, it is about being comfortable in their skin and with who they are. Knowing where your talents are and having plenty of opportunity to experience those talents are very important. When a child feels good about their musical talents, it is easier for them to not feel bad about their inability to catch a football. However, if they are put in situation after situation where they feel judged by their lack of physical agility, then this can cause a problem with their development of self-worth. It is important to see their unique gifts and to honor and help them develop those unique gifts. Because sensitive children feel things on such a deep level, they will also feel the joy of being themselves on a very deep level.

And the last place where we develop our self-esteem is with our intellect. When a child struggles to keep up with their peers academically, it is hard for them to develop a good sense of self. Unfortunately, our schools set these children up for failure. For children who learn differently, forming good self-esteem around intellect is very difficult. What we want to keep in mind is that learning differently does not mean inability to learn. However, a sensitive child who feels things deeply will often struggle with feeling smart and stupid at the same time. Deep inside, they know they are smart, but when they go to school, their external circumstances tell a different story. It is important for these children to be able to experience success. It is also important for them to realize that there is more than academic learning to intelligence. Imagination, problem-solving, and the ability to recognize a situation that requires their assistance or emotional intelligence are also forms of intelligence.

Every child has their own special superpowers, and helping them find what theirs are within each of the above areas of self-esteem will help them build their own unique brand of self-confidence.

Celebration Instead of Correction

If we can spend more time celebrating a child's awesomeness, we will automatically see that child gravitating towards behaviors and successes that display their awesomeness. The more we honor and celebrate the positive, the less need there will be to correct and criticize. Now, that doesn't mean we just let our children run amuck without any guidance. On the contrary, guidance along with consistent boundaries are very important. Healthy boundaries can help a child feel safe and encourage confidence. We get into trouble when we try to mold our children in a way that goes against their natural gifts. An example would be if a boy feels an inner sense of joy and freedom when he dances or performs, yet he is rewarded only for his athletic accomplishments while engaging in sports. He is told over and over again that sports will open all kinds of doors for him, such as social experiences and paying for college. Yet, in his heart, he knows that dancing and singing is what fulfills him. His mind is filled with all the shoulds and the whys, and his heart is left feeling empty.

A less obvious example would be a child who is very sensitive and caring towards others, a child who takes on the burdens of those around them, who feels the pain and sadness of world events, and who appears overly sensitive and cries over what appears as "just the little things." A boy may be told things such as "boys don't cry," "you need to be tougher," "crying is a sign of weakness," and "you won't get anywhere in life if you let people see your weakness." A girl may hear, "grow up," "don't be a baby," "you're crying for no reason," and "you need to be stronger or people will walk all over you." Comments like these don't honor a sensitive child's true nature. They tell a child that there must be something wrong with them because of the way they feel. It conveys weakness and vulnerability and devalues what they are feeling. Honoring a child's sensitivity as a true gift and then giving them tools they can use to navigate through life would allow a sensitive child to grow up with a healthy sense of self, inner strength, and confidence in following their own inner guidance system. Helping them to learn to trust their emotions is the key. Trying to change who they are at their core only causes them to devalue themselves and experience feelings of worthlessness. Feeling confident and valued is the right every child has, and this only comes by allowing each one of us to develop our own unique sense of self with our own sense of purpose.

Trying to make all of our kids fit into a box, that up until now society has accepted, is no longer going to suffice. Parents are starting to see this. They are standing up for their children and advocating for them. But this can be a very long and frustrating battle. Yes, seeing our children's gifts does start with a paradigm shift through our own eyes as parents, but without the schools stepping up to the plate and pitching in, our children will continue to struggle and be misunderstood. As children begin to see their own strength in their diversity, so will society begin to understand and shift the old paradigm.

Internal and External Intellect

We cast value on people based on what society says is important. One example that we see every day and especially in our schools is that of intellect. We place far too much value on intellect or at least on what most people consider intellect. Today, we live in a world that has so much information at our finger tips that we no longer have to rely on filling our heads up with specific types of knowledge. If we have a question, we can simply type it into an internet search engine to find the answer. The main problem here is that we look at intellectual status based on an old paradigm of external intellect. Our schools are set up to value external intellect, but what about internal intellect? We would have so many more gifted and creative people in the world if we would just honor intellectual diversity and begin teaching to our children's strengths, including that of internal intellect. Knowledge is a good thing, but knowledge comes from two different sources: external circumstances and inner knowing.

External knowledge or intellect is what has been programmed into us. This knowledge includes our academic teachings as well as our belief systems that we have adopted from external sources. This knowledge helps us tell time, read, do math, and other important skills that are needed in order to connect us to this physical world and with society. The thoughts that come from external sources are what help us develop this kind of intellect. Internal knowledge, or inner intellect, comes from within. It is the inner knowing of what is right and what is wrong, which does not follow any external rules. It is our ability to problem solve, create, and feel on a deep inner level. The thoughts that come from our inner knowing allow us to develop this kind of knowledge.

External intellect at one time did have its place, but today I believe that internal intellect is fast becoming the new normal and is a gift that should be honored and valued. External intellect comes from the mind and the ability to think, and yes, it is still a very valuable skill. Internal intellect comes from the heart and is the ability to feel and know from a deeper part of ourselves. This is what so many children today are gifted in. It's the ability to look beyond our present external circumstances and connect with a truth that goes beyond what we can see or hear with our physical senses. It's what an artist such as Michelangelo saw when he looked at a block of marble and saw *David* inside. His physical eyes and mind saw a block of marble, but his internal eyes, his heart, saw *David*, and he knew all he had to do was chip away at what did not belong.

Genius from the Heart

If you have ever watched one of those singing contests such as *American Idol* or the *Voice*, then you know that there are many talented singers out there. When it comes to technical singers, there is no shortage of natural talent. But heart is what separates one talented singer from the rest of the pack. Their natural ability to connect with a song, connect with their audience, and connect with their own true authenticity is genius that comes from their heart. In fact, the mind only gets in the way when it comes to an artist connecting with their music or their fans. Have you ever wondered why the winners of these shows are not always the singers that are the most technical? The winners are those who are able to develop a true connection with their music, their fans, and their own authenticity. In fact, connecting with your heart is what will set you apart from the pack in just about any career. Athletes, actors, doctors, teachers, cashiers, or any person in any career will truly shine when they are able to make a true connection with their heart and the people they serve.

So why are we not teaching this in our classrooms, our meeting rooms, and our homes? True genius comes from the ability to connect with the heart. So many of our children today are being born with this inner strength of knowing and seeing the world differently. They are more in touch with their inner knowing than ever before. Sure, we have seen many individuals throughout history, and adults today, who are more connected to this inner knowing, but my point here is that more and more children today are being born with this special superpower. Human evolution requires this strength, and today more and more people are working hard to develop this form of knowledge. It is not an easy journey for most of us due to the external programming that we have accepted as truth. However, I believe today's youth are coming in to this world with this built-in strength already developed at a heightened level, and helping them maintain and grow this inner strength is one of the most important things we can do for our youth today. I believe that it is time that we start valuing and honoring these inner strengths so that our children can grow up knowing what their superpower is and feel proud of it instead of feeling as if it is something that needs to be hidden or changed.

Internal intellect is what parents see in their children in the early stages of their development. Every parent knows this feeling of thinking how smart their child is when they say certain phrases or do certain things that appear to be beyond what they "should" be capable of. Many parents have reported to me throughout the years that they truly believed that their children were super intelligent before starting school, just to be shockingly surprised when the teachers in the first or second grades started to report on the challenges their children were displaying. In school, children are graded and compared to other children based on external learning, and in the process, their internal knowledge is unrecognized and not valued. With many children, this causes an internal battle in which they feel smart and stupid at the same time. They are out of sync with who they are, which causes a multitude of emotions to get bottled up and stuck inside of them. Helping these children release these emotions is very important to their emotional well-being. Not allowing these emotions to be released can cause anxiety, feelings of helplessness, and low self-esteem.

The best scenario is one in which these children feel valued right from the start and grow up in an environment where their superpowers are made visible and honored. By giving value to the internal intellect, children will be free to develop and grow within a paradigm that fits who they are at their core. In turn, society benefits from these changes as our children learn how best to develop their unique superpower, and the world learns how to honor the unique path that each of us is on. As we move away from the old paradigm and closer to the new paradigm, as society begins to embrace cooperation instead of competition, and as our children grow and develop a more compassionate way of seeing the world and each other, humanity will continue to evolve toward a more peaceful and harmonious way of being.

Out with the Old, in with the New

Change is happening. It may seem as if it is happening way too slowly, but as more and more people become aware of these changes, the old worldview will be replaced with the new and improved worldview. Our children are leading this change. Learning to see the beauty in each and every child begins with seeing what is already there. It's time we stop looking for what's wrong and start focusing on what's right. It's time our schools honor our child's differences and create programs that honor and value all of our children. The more we focus on the beauty within each child as parents, as friends, as educators, and as advocates, then the worldview will begin to change. Each step in this process will bring us closer to a society that values diversity and cooperation. Each of us can play our own part in this process.

More and more parents are beginning to understand this, which is why it has become increasingly more difficult for parents to just sit back quietly and follow the status quo. More and more educators are also recognizing and honoring the beautiful gifts that each of our children have been blessed with and are doing their best to unwrap them, but our present education system is making this nearly impossible. More and more private schools and charter schools are being created to find the ways to honor our children and their beautiful diversity, and they are proving that it can be done. When we begin to understand and see the beauty within a sensitive child, we can't help but know that this is truly an upgrade propelling humanity into a more caring, cooperative society.

Key Messages: Unwrapping Society

» Sensitivity is a beautiful gift that unfortunately society has portrayed as a weakness.

» Many children today can be described as being highly sensitive and may or may not have a developmental delay.

» Our world today needs more compassion and more empathy.

» Sensitivity is a beautiful gift that our world needs more of. Highly sensitive children tend to be creative and should be encouraged to think outside of the box.

» Many of history's great humanitarians are considered to have been highly sensitive, such as Mother Teresa and Martin Luther King Jr.

» Highly sensitive children feel and think more deeply.

» Highly sensitive children are very good at observation and will process and reflect upon what they see and hear on a very deep level.

» Being in nature can be very calming for a highly sensitive child.

» Sensitive children can have a harder time developing a good self-esteem.

» Building a strong sense of self comes from four main areas: family experiences, social experiences, physical experiences, and intellectual or academic experiences.

» Every child has their own unique superpowers, and helping them to find and cultivate theirs will help in developing good, strong self-esteem.

» Spend more time celebrating a child's awesomeness.

» Help a child learn that they can trust their emotions instead of fearing their emotions.

» Honor both external and internal intellect.

» Natural talent is common, but when it is paired with heart, it stands apart from the pack.

» As we move away from the old societal paradigm of competition to a new societal paradigm based in cooperation, humanity will continue to evolve toward a more peaceful society.

» It's time we stop looking for what is wrong and start focusing on what is right.

» The old paradigm is mind-based and the new paradigm is heart-based.

Old Paradigm	New Paradigm
Mind-Based *They are ruled by their thoughts that are based on old societal beliefs.*	**Heart-Based** *They follow guidance that comes from their heart and an inner knowing of what is right.*
In the Box *Fits in a box nicely and neatly. If they do not fit, then we will mold and shape them until they do fit.*	**Out of the Box** *They do not fit in a box, so we allow them to create and design a new box that fits them just right.*
Inside the Lines *Colors within the lines. If they go outside the lines, they will be corrected and taught the correct way of doing things.*	**Outside the Lines** *They color outside the lines, and they are encouraged to explore and create what they are feeling in their heart.*
Shoulds *They are taught what they should be doing.*	**Coulds** *They are encouraged to believe in what is possible.*
Conformity *They choose to wear a mask that presents themselves in a way that they have been taught to be.*	**Authenticity** *They are happy being exactly who they are. They are living an authentic life, experiencing the freedom of being themselves.*

One Size Fits All Academics	Teach to Strengths Academics
They are expected to learn a particular curriculum, and if they struggle keeping up with their peers, they are labeled and given services to help them keep up.	*They are taught to their strengths and placed in an environment that allows them to be successful. They are honored for their gifts and proud of who they are.*
Physical Development *They come into the world with an inner connection, but it is quickly lost.* *Their physical senses are connecting and organizing to the physical world, while their inner senses disconnect and forget.* *Their development is compared to statistical data that has been collected in the past.* *Dominant physical development is encouraged.*	**Inner Development** *Their inner senses are heightened and more strongly connected to their inner world.* *They are encouraged to maintain a strong connection with their inner senses as they grow and develop their connections with the outer world.* *Their development may be considered delayed compared to the old statistical data.* *Balance and harmony between the outer and the inner is encouraged.*

Strength	Sensitivity
They are taught to be strong and not show their emotions, since showing their emotions would be a sign of weakness.	They are taught that true strength comes from their ability to feel and connect with others with empathy and kindness.
Competition	Cooperation
They believe that they have to be better than others in order to succeed.	They know that everyone has their own unique awesomeness and being exactly who they are is perfect.
Limited Resources	Shared Resources
They believe that they need to work harder and faster than others in order to get a bigger piece of the pie.	They know that there is plenty to go around, and through cooperation and support of others, everyone will prosper.
Force	Power
They are taught to push and push until they get what they want. They are taught that hard work pays off.	They know that true strength comes from within, and they are confident in following their own inner knowing.

External Guidance	Internal Guidance
They look at external circumstances to guide themselves in their decision-making.	*They trust their inner knowing in order to guide themselves in their decision-making.*
Values External Strength	**Values Internal Strength**
Intelligence is measured by external programming.	*Intelligence is measured by an internal knowing.*
Individual Focus	**Collective Focus**
They put themselves first and live by the belief that it is a "dog eat dog world."	*They realize that we are all connected, and they thrive in environments of cooperation.*

CHAPTER 6

Unwrapping Parenting

*Understanding the competitive forces that
drive modern-day parenting and the ways to
move towards cooperation*

We live in a society based on a competitive paradigm, which has greatly affected the way we raise our children. As parents, we often take on the role of CEO in our child's life. It's not our fault, it's just that we have inherited the belief that it is our job to shape and mold our children in a way that is most conducive to fitting into today's society. We are conditioned to look for weaknesses, and we believe it is our job to fix those weaknesses. We watch our children carefully, comparing them to other children and to normative data we collect from our pediatrician's office and from online sources. We may not always admit it, but in those early years, we are looking for signs that our child is outperforming other children. We want them to be smarter, faster, taller, cuter, and whatever else we may value as important. Deep down, we know that having a healthy happy child is most important, yet we still often treat parenting as if it was a competitive sport. Why is this? Because we are all living within a social paradigm that values these attributes. We make our parenting decisions based on external sources that society has accepted as important. More specifically, we have been living in a competitive paradigm where getting there first is better than last and where having more is better than less. We believe that there is not enough to go around, so you have to outplay and outsmart everyone in order to be successful. This is the paradigm that humanity has been caught up in for centuries, and we pass these beliefs down from generation to generation.

But what if it is not true? What if there is plenty to go around? What would the world look like if instead of living within a competitive paradigm, we lived within a new paradigm based on cooperation? What if the truth is actually that every one of us is of equal value and that no one is better or worse than another? What if our diversity is actually where our true strength lies? Within a cooperative society, everyone would be valued for their own unique gifts. I believe that the world needs to transition to a more cooperative paradigm in order to survive, and I believe that this is where we are headed.

Today, we are still passing along the old beliefs that we have inherited, but something is vastly different. The old paradigm is no longer serving children of today. They are evolving and are not able to thrive within the old competitive paradigm. They no longer fit into the status quo. More and more children are feeling as if they don't fit in at all. They are becoming more sensitive and have a stronger connection with their inner senses, which is what connects all of us with the heart.

From Competition to Cooperation

Albert Einstein said, "The most important decision we make is whether we believe we live in a friendly or a hostile universe." Well, I believe we live in a friendly universe, and I believe that humanity is constantly evolving toward a more peaceful and harmonious world. I believe that the future of humanity is dependent upon our ability to evolve into a more cooperative and compassionate society, and I believe our children are evolving in order to fulfill this need. More and more children today are coming into this world with stronger inner senses, which is why so many children are being seen as extra sensitive. I have seen this change over the years in my practice, and I have heard it over and over again from parents and professionals working with children. More and more children today are processing the world differently, and therefore, we need to take a good look at what we are teaching them. When we try to program this new and improved operating system (today's children) with old outdated software (the old paradigm), then we end up with a mismatch that can lead to overwhelm and frustration. When we take into consideration how a child may be perceiving the world differently, then we can understand how we may be able to help them by simply making a few adjustments to their environment. For example, let's look at how Anna was helped once mom started to understand Anna's different way of processing the world and began parenting using a cooperative paradigm. In other words, she began working with Anna's gifts by honoring her different needs.

Anna was extremely sensitive, which her parents described as being overly sensitive. Based on their old paradigm, they believed that Anna's sensitivity was a problem, and they did not know what to do to help her. She often had meltdowns and would easily shut down. Often, when they were trying to help her, they would become frustrated with her apparent lack of effort. She would often become very upset when seeing homeless people on the street, since she was picking up on the emotions from the people around her. She felt genuine empathy for the homeless people that she would see, and she was actually taking on their emotions. When she was bombarded by so many emotions at once, it would become very hard to tell what belonged to her and what emotions belonged to everyone else. Anna's parents needed to work with Anna's emotions, allow her to feel what she needed to feel, and create a place where she could recharge and feel safe.

Mom decided to create a tent over her bed, and this became a place where Anna would go whenever she needed to block out the crazy energies around her and ground herself. Mom started to talk with Anna about the homeless people, and together they worked out a way that they could help by putting together food bags to distribute and ordering school supplies for children who couldn't afford them. Anna's parents began cooperating within her unique way of seeing and perceiving the world instead of judging and trying to change her behavior. They changed the way they saw her and began participating with her in ways that helped her to feel safe. Very quickly, they started to notice improvement in Anna's compliance with fewer meltdowns and less frustration. They also started to see improvement in her reading and, more importantly, a willingness to try even if she was still struggling. All in all, Anna was much happier, less frustrated, and her academics were even improving. Once Anna's parents began looking toward their own hearts for guidance in how to help their daughter, Anna blossomed.

By observing the beautiful sensitive heart of her child, Anna's mom was able to rediscover her own knowing of how to help her daughter. By not looking at the external world for guidance, she turned her attention inward and was guided by her own heart on what to do. With this, mom's frustration level significantly reduced, Anna's frustration level in response was significantly reduced, and in turn, dad began to notice the difference and also reduced his level of frustration. By first understanding, then accepting, and finally implementing the necessary changes, Anna's parents were able to create both an external environment (tents and creative ways of helping people) and, more importantly, an internal environment (their own thoughts and feelings) that was more conducive to the way Anna perceives the world.

The first step is understanding how your child's senses are perceiving the world, not only on a physical level but also on a metaphysical or energetic level. Next, you want to help them to feel safe within the parameters of their sensory needs. Give them a space to recharge and ground themselves when they need to, such as building a tent or providing them with a quiet, soothing area. This can also include therapies or programs that are designed to help specific sensory areas balance and develop more harmonious connections.

It is important not only to help connect and balance the physical senses but to also help them balance and develop their inner senses. There are many sensory integration programs available today provided by occupational therapists and physical therapists specializing in sensory integration that focus on balancing and developing the physical senses; however, they tend to ignore the importance of balancing and developing the inner senses.

Advice for the Parent

Here are some ways in which you can help your child balance and develop their inner senses:

- Don't simply dismiss what they are feeling. If you value their feelings, then they will learn to value their feelings and not feel the need to hide them.

- Help them learn to listen to their heart and to trust their heart. Teach them to follow their own inner guidance system and not the crowd. Learning to trust their own inner knowing will help them to feel safe when they are being bombarded by so many mixed emotions. Help them to get quiet and know the difference between outer beliefs and their inner knowing.

- Spend more time celebrating their wins. One way of doing this is by setting time aside everyday, perhaps at bedtime, to talk about their day and to acknowledge the wins of the day. At first, this may be a little challenging, but after a while you will find that it becomes easy; eventually, identifying and celebrating their wins will become habit. For example, getting dressed on their own, remembering to bring their lunch to school, and helping out a friend are all worth celebrating. The wins can include academic wins, but focusing on their areas of strength will help them to be comfortable and accepting of their own true awesomeness.

- Talk openly about their superpowers and find time each day to discuss examples of when they were using these superpowers.

- Help them to see that they can be compassionate and caring without having to take on the feelings and emotions of others. It is also helpful to explore what other people are feeling or might be feeling in order to help them establish that feelings are unique to each of us. Without judgement, honor what others may or may not be feeling.

- Know it's not your job to change them; it's just your job to love them and help guide them on the path of loving themselves. This is sometimes difficult when they are constantly having outer experiences of struggle and failure, which often happens in school. The more they feel your love without feelings of judgement or disappointment, the easier it will be for them to grow up loving who they are instead of trying so hard to be someone they are not.

- Move from fear and hopelessness to love and hopefulness. By spending more time focusing on their wins, their gifts, and their awesomeness, you will find that your positive thoughts will result in more positive emotions.

- Talk to them openly, and allow them to safely express their feelings and their emotions without judgement. It is important to let them know that you are there for them without judging them. They are more affected by what is happening to them and by what is happening in the world. They can feel fear and sadness toward tragic events, such as natural disasters. Helping them to feel safe can be a challenge today, especially with so many tragedies happening in the world.

• Give them a place to dump, recharge, and ground themselves when they need to. Create space for them to get away from overstimulation. Highly sensitive children need down time to help them recover and feel grounded when there is too much stimulation going on around them. It is common for a sensitive child to get overwhelmed easily. The most important thing to keep in mind is that what they are feeling is real, and it is okay for them to have those feelings.

• Provide opportunities to get them involved in community service. Help them to discover ways in which they can be of service to others and develop their natural empathic nature. Show them that you honor and support them. Teach them how important it is to accept the quirks and differences in others. This will also help them accept it in themselves.

• Encourage curiosity. Help them to be seekers and question-askers. Questioning the why and encouraging curiosity will help to develop a child's natural desire for knowledge.

- Encourage imaginative play. Helping a child to cultivate their natural imagination is another way of building social and emotional skills, language skills, thinking and problem-solving skills. Role playing, for example, is a good way for children to exercise listening skills and empathy-building skills.

- Be mindful of your reactions, especially negative ones. Remember, highly sensitive children can often feel what other people are feeling. They may pick up on your disappointments, fears, and insecurities. They may need help sorting through their feelings in order to figure out what belongs to them and what belongs to others. It is very common for sensitive children to take on what others are feeling, so help them to release what does not belong to them.

- Take care of yourself. Taking care of your own needs is not selfish; in fact, it is very important that you take care of yourself so that you are not feeling drained, since this can cause your child to become drained. Be a good role model of self-care for your child who is highly sensitive. They will learn from what you model, so taking care of yourself first is very important in order to teach them how to take care of themselves. Highly sensitive people tend to become great caregivers but often neglect to take care of themselves.

- Show your love. The most important thing for a highly sensitive child to feel is love. Knowing that they are loved and valued for who they are will help them to grow up feeling good about who they are with a healthy self-esteem. Self-love comes from feeling loved by others. If a child does not feel loved for who they are, it is extremely difficult for them to grow up loving themselves.

Parenting a highly sensitive child is an extremely important job. Since they feel things on such a deep level, love and nurture become vitally important. When a sensitive child grows up knowing that they are loved for who they are, they will be more likely to feel safe and confident. They will feel free to be exactly who they are without having to wear a mask. They will be more likely to lead a successful life and will be able to recover more quickly from life's setbacks. On the other hand, when a highly sensitive child grows up with feelings of not being safe and feeling afraid, they will be less likely to venture out. They will be less likely to let their true essence be seen. They will be more apt to hide themselves so that they are not found out. They are more likely to feel self-conscious with a low self-esteem. They will be more prone to substance abuse and depression.

Our world has been blessed with so many beautiful children today who are more sensitive and more compassionate than ever before. This is a beautiful gift for humanity, but it is so important that these gifts are nurtured and honored so they can expand. When we are able to see a child's differences through loving eyes instead of fearful eyes, the entire paradigm will shift. As we begin to see beyond the external weaknesses and embrace the internal strength, then more and more children will grow into their awesomeness, lighting this world up with their grace. In time, this will create societal change and acceptance of a new social consciousness. We are already seeing how much impact our youth can have today. The events following the Stoneman Douglas High School shooting and the "March for Our Lives" demonstrations around the country suggest that today's youth will stop at nothing to bring about change with a compassionate heart, inner courage, and strength. True courage, strength, and power come from within. Shame, criticism, and judgement come from outside.

The old paradigm is one in which we are constantly focused on looking for red flags or searching for potential problems. We spend more time looking for problems then we do celebrating when things are going well. As a society, we are always quick to point out or correct the negative but are not as likely to point out or celebrate the positive. In doing this, we often miss out on wonderful opportunities to celebrate a child's awesomeness. It can be very frustrating and overwhelming when a child does not seem to fit the old mold, when they overreact emotionally or when they have trouble coping with normal everyday experiences. Helping our children begins by looking beyond the physical and looking inward at how they are perceiving not just the physical world differently but also how their inner senses are perceiving the world differently.

The old competitive paradigm that parents have adopted in the past is no longer serving our children of today, who will thrive within a new paradigm based in cooperation. This means that we work within the parameters of their ever-changing and ever-evolving sensory processing system and help them find harmony and balance between the physical senses and the senses that go beyond the physical. Helping them find balance with their mind-based thoughts and their heart-based thoughts is essential in helping them thrive and create a new world with a new paradigm. Humanity desperately needs more sensitive, caring, empathic people in order to evolve into a more compassionate and cooperative society. It is so important that we help nurture these gifts that so many of our children are being blessed with today.

Acknowledging the Challenge

To all the parents out there who think no one is listening, I want you to know that I am listening, and it is time that more people hear your cries so that we can have real change for all our children.

Here are some of the things I have heard parents say to me.

- I'm tired of fighting for every little thing that my child needs.

- Nobody should ever leave a school meeting and then sit in the parking lot for an hour crying.

- Why doesn't anyone understand that my child is smart, they just learn differently than other children?

- Why can't they learn to teach to my child in the way that they learn?

- I don't love the school system, but I love any teacher who is able to see my beautiful child and her beautiful brain.

- I have spent years trying to figure it out and then years trying to explain it to people. Why is it so hard to get people to listen?

- I vacillate between anger and sadness, and somewhere in between is helplessness.

- How can you have a child with a problem and not be able to find anyone who is able to help you fix it, or at least be willing to work with you in order to figure it out together?

- I am not looking for perfect. I just want my child to feel that they are perfect already.

- My child does not have to be like everyone else, I just want them to feel good about being who they are.

Parenting alone is challenging enough, but when you throw in challenges such as anxiety disorder, social emotional disorder, ADD/ADHD, sensory or auditory processing disorder, or any other processing disorder, then you have just cranked up the difficulty level tenfold. There are quite simply no words that can adequately describe the emotional rollercoaster that these parents are on every day. As parents, it is very easy to get caught up in the idea that our children are here to learn from us, and therefore we spend a lot of time in our heads trying to figure out what is best for them. We put a lot of effort into how best to mold them into fitting into society. We become concerned with how they are perceived by others and therefore become easily overwhelmed when things don't seem to be going the way we think they should. In fact, it sometimes feels that worrying about our kids is just part of the job description, and believe me, it does not stop once they are all grown up. I still worry about my adult daughter every day.

But what if the main purpose of having children is so that we can learn from them? What if every perceived challenge is a chance for us to shine the light on something inside of us that wants to be revealed? Looking within ourselves for the answers just may be the greatest challenge of all. Maybe we are not here to change them, but maybe they are here to change us, to help us look inside of ourselves and become the observer of our own feelings and emotions so that we can grow and develop into the highest and best versions of who we are here to be.

Our feelings and our emotions serve as our guideposts on this journey we call life. Learning to connect and use this built-in navigation system is something we are born with, but most of us lose touch with it as we grow up and connect to more of the external circumstances that we are repeatedly exposed to. However, as many of us have discovered, nothing stirs up more emotions in us than our children. From the very highest of highs from watching their first smile to their first steps, we watch in anticipation of each and every accomplishment. We celebrate with them in a way no one else can. We also feel their pain in a way no one else possibly can. Watching your child struggle can be more painful than actually going through the same challenges yourself.

Every experience we have elicits an emotion, and our emotions are here to guide us on our own personal journey of self-development. So, what better way to accelerate that journey than to enhance those emotions by attaching the parent-child bond. We are all here on our own personal journey. Learning to honor that path is a courageous step in the right direction of fulfilling our purpose.

Love, Find, Focus

This is an exercise that will help you adjust your focus throughout the day in a loving way instead of in a fearful way.

1. Take a sheet of paper, and draw a line down the middle of the page from the top to the bottom.

2. At the top, label the left side with "Fear" and the right side with "Love."

3. Now, start writing in the left column all the things you can think of that cause you to be concerned about your child. Write the things that keep you up at night worrying and all the things that you are afraid other people think about your child.

4. Now, on the right side, start listing all the awesome things about your child. List everything about them that you see in your heart. List all the things you know about them that you wish others would see. List all their superpowers, all their physical attributes that you adore, and all their inner attributes that make them so beautiful and special. Write as much as you can but know you can add to it later.

Notice which list was easier to add things to. Notice how you feel when you are adding to the fear side and when you are adding to the love side. Notice how you feel when you read from the different columns. Then, throughout the next few days, notice how often you are having fear-based thoughts that are on the list and how often you are having love-based thoughts that are on the list. Once you have had a chance to observe your thoughts, and how often you are on the left side of the list and how often you are on the right side of the list, then you can start directing your thoughts to the right side. Redirecting your thoughts from the fear-based to love-based will have a dramatic change in the way you see your child, and more importantly, in the way that they see themselves. I promise you, this really works, so give it a try and you will start to see things change immediately.

Key Messages: Unwrapping Parenting

» Within a cooperative society, everyone is valued for their own unique gifts.

» The old competitive paradigm does not support children of today.

» Sensitive children thrive within a cooperative environment.

» A child needs to feel safe within the parameters of how they are processing the world.

» Value your child's feelings, honor how they are feeling, and help them to release what does not belong to them.

» Help them to listen to their own inner knowing and to trust it.

» Spend time everyday celebrating your child's wins.

» It's not your job to change your child; it is your job to love them and help them to unwrap their authenticity.

» Give them space to dump and recharge when they are feeling overwhelmed.

» Encourage curiosity and imagination.

» Take care of yourself and model positive self-care.

» Always show them that you love them and that they are not their behavior.

» Sensitivity needs to be nurtured and cultivated so that it can develop and expand.

» Helping our children begins by looking beyond the physical and looking inward at how they are perceiving the world around them.

» Humanity desperately needs more sensitive, caring, empathic people in order to evolve into a more compassionate and cooperative society.

» Maybe we are not here to change our children; maybe they are here to change us.

CHAPTER 7

Unwrapping Schools

Understanding the school system's failing
model and the steps we can take to change it

It is not a mistake that so many children today are struggling in school and that so-called developmental delays are on the rise. It's a beautiful transformation that we are witnessing, but it is essential that we embrace and honor neurodiversity and the different ways that so many of our children today are processing the world. It is time that we reevaluate our educational system. We can't stop our children from changing, but we can change the way we are educating them. We have been trying to "fix" our children for years now, and it's not working. In fact, the situation is getting worse, which is quite evident in the ongoing rise of drug and alcohol abuse, self-injury, suicide, and school shootings today. I believe that it is no coincidence that more and more of these tragic events are occurring. More and more children are being placed in environments that are not conducive to their way of learning. More and more children are feeling socially isolated and don't feel as if they "fit in." Today's children do not and will not thrive within a competitive paradigm. It goes against their nature. Their nature is to include, not separate, and to follow their heart, not the crowd. They are true to who they are at their core and have a much stronger knowing of what is right and what is wrong than ever before.

When these children are placed in an environment that does not support this new way of being, the result is misalignment and imbalance. They feel lost and out of sync with who they are. They feel things so much deeper than ever before, which is why their behaviors are often more extreme than ever before. In a competitive environment, these children are not able to connect easily with others, which goes against their true nature. This causes deep feelings of isolation, along with feelings of unworthiness. In a competitive environment, they are not in harmony with their true nature. They are not able to feel safe. Cooperation is essential for sensitive people to feel safe. Cooperation feeds their empathic heart and their need to be in harmony with each other. This is what needs to change. Changing our children is not an option; changing our belief system and our educational system is the answer. Schools are where our children spend most of their time and where they form much of their self-image. Even if a child comes from a loving and caring home, spending six hours a day in a setting where they feel different or less than their peers will supersede any positive belief system that they may be learning at home.

Our Failing School Systems

It is essential that children form a strong, healthy self-image of themselves early on in order to grow up to be healthy, positive adult members of society. With the way most of our schools are set up today, this is not happening. There are many reasons for this, one being the competitive nature of our society and, therefore, of our schools. Schools are being compared to one another based on test scores and performance of their students. This competition trickles down from administration to teachers and ultimately to our students. Schools compete with each other for funding, teachers compete with each other just to keep their jobs, and students are taught to compete with each other so that they can get into the best schools, get the best jobs, and be better than everyone else. In keeping with our societal belief of competition as a model, schools have come up with a set of standards with the goal of forcing our children to perform within those standards. Where did these standards come from? Who decided that every child should learn the same things, in the same way, and at the same time?

This just simply does not work. It's like building a puzzle where the hole is the same round shape, and all the different puzzle pieces are being forced to fit into that round hole. What happens is that some pieces fit easily through that hole, so they get in first and feel really good about themselves. Other pieces have to be changed, perhaps shaving parts of themselves away in order to fit through the hole. They make it in, but now they have had to learn how to be something they are not. Some of them may manage to adapt eventually and wear the mask that fools people into thinking that they are fitting in. But on the inside, they never really feel right. They have lost who they are in the process of trying to fit in and, therefore, have lost their authenticity. This group will spend much of their life out of harmony with who they are. They grow up lost, searching for themselves. Some manage to reconnect with their true self somewhere along their journey, while others just may stay lost throughout their lifetime.

Then there is the third group who just can't fit through the hole no matter how much they are reshaped. The system is trying desperately to reshape them, cutting here and squishing there, but no matter how much reshaping is done, they just never fit through that hole. Eventually, the system gives up on them and settles for leaving them out. They create another box where all the misfit pieces can go, and they clear their consciences by accepting that there is simply something wrong with those pieces or that external circumstances such as poor parenting are to blame. This is the educational paradigm that we are placing our children in. With overcrowded classrooms, teachers can't possibility teach to each child. Those who don't fit or can't conform simply get left behind. Sure, we create legislation such as No Child Left Behind Act and Every Student Succeeds Act, but we're basing these changes on principles from the old paradigm, and these changes are simply not working. It's time we start to look at our children differently and begin honoring who they are instead of trying to make them fit in.

Change is happening in a big way, and as with any change, we will experience growing pains. When change happens as quickly as it seems to be happening now, the growing pains are equally as challenging. If you don't change with it, you will get swallowed up by it. Today, we see change happening in the way we shop, the way we listen to music, watch TV, travel, worship, communicate, and socialize. Malls and stores are being replaced by online shopping. Music, movies, and TV are now being downloaded through the internet. People book their own travel through online sites. They maintain relationships through social media and cell phones. They worship without going to church, and they speak to each other without speaking. Those who adapt and change will be able to thrive, and those who don't adapt won't thrive.

With all this change that is happening around us, why are our schools so determined to hold on to an old paradigm that is not working and is no longer serving such a large percentage of our children? Today's schools have become the race track to academic learning, where the arts are slowly becoming nearly nonexistent. When I was in school, kindergarten was where most children started school and where we were taught cooperative play. Today, most children go to preschool and are expected to be pre-reading if not already reading by the time they start kindergarten. In fact, there are many communities where parents are encouraged to hold their children back a year before starting kindergarten in order to give them a head start. Our societal belief is one of competition, and therefore our schools have taken on that role as well. Schools are becoming more and more competitive with each other and are encouraging a competitiveness within the school that places child against child, further resulting in competitiveness among parents. This needs to change, or more and more of our children are going to be lost because of it.

Why are more and more families feeling the need to homeschool their children instead of receiving an appropriate education from our "free" educational system? Why are so many families feeling the need to fight the school system in order to get what they feel is the right education for their child? Why are so many teachers frustrated with overcrowded classrooms and policies that no longer allow them to teach? Most importantly, why are so many children not able to succeed within the typical classroom, and why is our school system failing so many of our children today? The answer was not found in the legislation of No Child Left Behind, and it is not going to be found in the Every

Student Succeeds Act either. Testing children will never be an accurate measurement of a student's learning, if we continue to educate them in the same manner. In fact, no testing will ever accurately measure performance, since there is so much diversity in the way each individual learns and in each child's natural gifts. It's time that our schools move away from the old competitive paradigm and create a new paradigm of cooperation that is more in alignment with today's sensitive child.

A New Education Model

The word education has two different Latin roots. One is "educare," which means to train or to mold, and the other is "educere," which means to lead out or draw out. There are many people who use these meanings to argue one side or the other. For instance, the first one suggests the passing down of knowledge, and shaping and molding our youth in the image of their parents and that of the past. This system uses rote memorization and models appropriate behavior. The second meaning has been used to argue that education should be to prepare a new generation for the future based on changes that are inevitable. This requires questioning, thinking, and the ability to create. Many argue that our schools should find a balance between these two ideas. What I would like to propose is that perhaps, in the past, it was necessary to mold and teach conformity, since it was part of the old paradigm. However, as I have been demonstrating here, the world is changing at a very rapid rate, and our youth today are leading the way on this path of change.

How about we create a new system that honors every child for who they are and lives by the model of "No Child Left Unwrapped," a model of education that honors the gifts every child is born with, a new paradigm where children are able to be comfortable being who they are instead of who they think they should be? It's time we spend more time looking at what each child is able to do instead of constantly focusing on what they can't do. Children would then grow up being proud of who they are. Their self-image would be preserved with an exuberant joy of being exactly who they are. With this paradigm, productivity would increase, creativity would be honored, and every child would then be able to truly succeed. What the world needs more of today are individuals who are kind, creative, and sensitive to the needs of others. We need more cooperation, not more competition, and a great place to start is with our schools. I believe that this is where we are headed with this new generation of individuals who are coming into this world more strongly connected to their inner senses than to their outer physical senses. This is a positive, not a negative. This is a gift that should be nurtured, not a defect that needs to be corrected. We are headed toward a world that is more directed by the heart than with the intellect, and emotional harmony is the key. Children today are capable of extreme empathy toward others, and feeling connected to others is extremely important to them. This is why a cooperative environment is so vitally important today.

As a collective, we will all benefit from a balanced world of equally important individuals, coming together to build a more caring peaceful society where everyone has a sense of belonging. Our children spend most of their time in school; therefore, if we can model a social environment of cooperation within our school system, then that is what we will be teaching them instead of a competitive "dog eat dog" society. I dream of a world where every child is taught their value, where every child is valued equally, where every child grows up knowing who they are at the very core of their being and that knowing makes them proud to be exactly who they are. And in this dream, these children grow up honoring diversity, living in harmony, and creating a new worldview based in cooperation. It's time we release the old paradigm of competition and begin structuring our society with examples of cooperation, starting with schools.

I have seen this repeatedly in my practice working with children with auditory processing disorder and other sensory processing challenges. I have heard from many teachers and therapists who simply just want to cast the children aside who do not learn like the other children or who present as not being motivated. It seems as if so many educators are just trying to "find a place" for many of our children within a system that is not meant for them, instead of really digging down and creating a new environment that would allow these children to be successful. The greatest value is being placed on the children who are able to thrive in the present educational system, and unfortunately it seems like fewer and fewer of our children are falling into this category. When I speak to therapists and teachers, I hear more and more about how so many more children are not succeeding and are requiring extra services. I have also heard from them that they are seeing a significant increase in children who are being described as extra sensitive. More and more parents are reporting to me that they see a special sensitive side to their children that really surprises them at times. The old paradigm worked in the past, but today's children need a new paradigm in order to thrive and develop the beautiful, unique gifts that live inside each of them.

Not only do today's children have difficulty adapting to wearing the different societal masks, but many have a deep knowing within of who they are and are refusing to wear the masks. This is evident with what is being seen in this country today with our young people standing up for their rights and for what they believe in at their very core. More and more young people are showing us their compassionate hearts with calls of love and cooperation. In this new world of cooperation, the old paradigms of our competitive political system, our competitive economic system, and our competitive educational system will no longer be supported. Perhaps it is time that we create a new model of our education system, one that better fits our new generation of creative, heart-based, empathic children. It's time we embrace our children with all the beautiful diversity that they are bringing into the world. They are here, and they are going to become who they are meant to be, whether or not we change with them. They are no longer going to conform to our model, so my suggestion is that we embrace change and begin to conform to who they are and to what they need, so they can move forward and create a more beautiful world—a world of cooperation, of love, of kindness, and of genuine concern for the whole.

> *"Where is the book in which the teacher can read about what teaching is? The children themselves are this book. We should not learn to teach out of any book other than the one lying open before us and consisting of the children themselves."*
> —Rudolf Steiner

One example of an educational model based on new paradigm ideals was developed by Rudolf Steiner, an Austrian philosopher, scientist, and artist of the late 19th century and early 20th century. He founded the Waldorf-Astoria school in 1919, and today there are approximately 1,000 Waldorf schools in 60 different countries. His educational philosophy was that teachers should not only focus on the physical needs of a student but that they should also focus on the emotional and spiritual needs of each child individually. He emphasized creativity and believed in the power of play. Rudolf Steiner's approach to teaching is a good example of looking beyond the physical and allowing a child to unfold and grow into the best version of themselves. The Waldorf method uses a whole child approach to learning, allowing each child's unique gifts to be unraveled and developed. It holds that a child's education should not be rushed and that there are specific developmental times in which academic learning should be introduced. The goal is to inspire lifelong learning and to teach a child from the inside out instead of from the outside in. In Rudolf Steiner's words, "The heart of the Waldorf method is the conviction that education is an art—it must speak to the child's experience. To educate the whole child, the heart and will must be reached as well as the mind."

Another educational model that embodies the principles of using creativity and allowing an individual's gifts to be cultivated and developed is that of "The Project Approach." In this model, children are guided through an in-depth investigation of real world topics. It provides a theoretical framework that works in conjunction with academic learning by including hands-on projects that allow for a multisensory approach to learning. It encourages all children with different strengths, weaknesses, interests, and backgrounds to come together in small groups and learn from an interactive approach. At the school my daughter attended, Progressive School of Long Island, their approach to education consists of co-teaching and small classrooms. Children are encouraged to work independently and at their own pace. They use a multisensory approach and place value on teaching the whole child by including physical, mental, and spiritual disciplines. By honoring diversity of learning, every child feels successful and valued for their own unique gifts.

What Education Is and Isn't Teaching Our Children

How we teach our children is not the only problem that our education system is facing today. It is important that we look at what we are teaching, or more importantly, what we are not teaching. It is for good reason that a large part of attention is placed on literacy within our education system. The ability to read and write is important for many different reasons. It also is the foundation that helps us to learn the other disciplines within our education system such as math, science, and history. As our society changes and our common needs adapt to our changing world, certain things become less important. For example, when my daughter was in school, she struggled with spelling. I was concerned that the school was not helping her with this, and I recall the director of the school telling me that he did not feel it was a skill she needed to learn because of technology and of the ability to use spell check.

On the other side, we now have classes teaching computer science, and we even use computers for teaching many subjects today. Technology is changing the way we teach and what we teach, however, there is something very important that is missing. We are living in a different world where technology is evolving rapidly, and this is creating some very unique challenges that, as a society, we have not faced before. We are also seeing children evolve in a way in which their sensory processing system is changing, and they are becoming more connected with their inner senses. These two factors have created a situation that desperately needs to be addressed. It is no longer enough that we focus education on the outer world. We must expand our education system to include helping our children cultivate and develop a better understanding of their inner world.

Technology has expanded our ability to connect and relate to one another regardless of our physical proximity to each other. It has also opened the door to sharing of knowledge. With so much external change happening in the world around us, and with all the inner changes we are seeing in the way so many of our children are processing the world, there is a greater need than ever before to educate our children differently. They need more than the tools of reading, writing, and communication skills that verbal language provides. They need a way to understand and question what is happening on a deeper level. They need to be taught a new set of skills that directly relate to human behavior.

Today, our children live in a world where the simple act of going to school is no longer safe. This is an unfortunate reality that we are facing today. I live very close to the Marjory Stoneman Douglas High School, where 17 individuals lost their lives earlier this year, and happened to be across the street from the school at the time of the horrible incident on February 14, 2018. Being so close to this tragedy and seeing the impact that it had on the surrounding communities, as well as across the country, I can't help but feel a very strong desire to stand up and to do something that can help bring positive change to a situation that is rapidly getting out of control. We desperately need a solution to this horrible trend we are seeing today, and I don't believe the solution will be found from gun control, arming teachers, beefing up security, or bullet-proofing our schools. These are all external solutions, and although they may be helpful, we cannot solve this problem unless we take into account that this is not just an external problem; we need to look more closely at the internal causes, too.

In our high-tech world, increasing gun control is not a viable solution when anyone can build their own weapon with a downloaded file from the internet and a 3-D printer. No, the answer to this problem is not going to be found when we look at it from the old paradigm of examining external circumstances. The solution will be found when we start looking within to prevent a child from feeling so desperate and so out of touch that they feel that their only option is to commit such a violent crime. The answer is not in arming our teachers with guns; the answer is in arming our students with a different kind of knowledge. The answer that I am talking about here can be found in what Paul Chappell calls "Peace Literacy." Paul is the director of the Nuclear Age Peace Foundation and the author of a seven-book series called *Road to Peace*. Peace literacy is a movement that provides students with training, tools, and information that get to the root of the problem. It is a program based on educating people on the basic needs of belonging and self-value. The program presents a new perspective on school bullying and what children can do instead of what they should not do. It teaches children about compassion, empathy, and how to be more respectful to others, explores why people behave in certain ways, and models ways in which students can become more reflective of their own behavior. I believe that Paul's message and his peace literacy framework for presenting this information into our schools is a positive step in the right direction to help make our schools safe and to teach our children from the inside-out perspective as well as from the outside-in perspective.

Our children aren't failing schools. Our schools are failing them. We have created one legislation after another trying to correct this problem, and it is time for real change. That change is not going to come from the old competitive paradigm or from tweaking or making meaningless changes. It's time to dismantle what is no longer serving our youth and build a system that supports and honors every child. I truly believe this can be done and desperately needs to be done, or our most valuable resource—our children—will be lost. It is very easy to look upon this enormous task and believe that it can't be done, but one of the things I have learned when taking on a big project is that it is best to look at the baby steps that are needed to get us closer to our ultimate goal. By focusing on the little steps and continuing to move forward, one step at a time, change will happen. When we look at the giant task ahead of us, it is far too easy to feel overwhelmed and to shut down, remaining stuck exactly where we are.

Steps towards a Better Future

Recently, I attended a service at the Unity Church of Pompano Beach and found myself engrossed by a sermon that was given by Rev. Lawrence Palmer. He told the story of the meaning behind Jesus's words, "No one puts new wine into old wineskins. If he does, the wine will burst the skins—and the wine is destroyed, and so are the skins. But new wine is for fresh wineskins." (Mark 2:22). In this passage, Jesus was trying to demonstrate that the old practice of fasting was a ritualistic practice that belonged to an old paradigm he believed no longer served. In other words, you can't put new ideas into old mindsets, and you can't get new results with old behaviors. This is a perfect example of how our children today are no longer being served by the old educational paradigm, and why it is so important that we create a new paradigm, one that is more appropriate for today's changing world and the children who are here to pave the path.

We have to move forward and change with them if we want them to thrive. The baby steps that we can focus on as teachers, therapists, advocates, and those who work closely with our children today include:

- Understanding and accepting the diversity within each and every child. This understanding begins by looking beyond the physical senses and acknowledging that there may be more than meets the eye, literally.

- Honoring the gifts that every child is born with. Within each of us is a perfection of genius wanting to be discovered and nurtured. Don't give up on a child just because their genius does not look like what you expect it to look like. Go beyond ordinary and discover the extraordinary potential that lives within everyone.

- Show them that you support them in their unique genius. Let them know that their awesomeness is valued just as much as anyone else's. The athlete, the mathlete, the musician, the computer nerd, everyone is equally valued and supported.

- Celebrate the wins no matter what they are. Develop the habit of looking through the lens of love in order to shine a light on each child's awesomeness.

- Set up an environment based on cooperation. Starting in the classroom, a new paradigm of cooperation can be demonstrated, leading the way toward discovery of the power of working together.

- Celebrate and explore diversity within the classroom or small group settings. Within a cooperative model, children can learn how each person contributes to the whole in their own unique way in order to make the whole stronger.

- Adopt an educational model that teaches compassion and empathy, such as the Peace Literacy model.

Competition has its place, and we don't want to throw out the baby with the bath water. Teach inner competition instead of external competition. Inner competition puts the focus on each of us to be the best we can be. From within, we can set goals and strive toward improvement without judging others or trying to overshadow others. There is a place for each of us to find our own success. By celebrating everyone's wins together in a classroom or small group, children will learn that everyone's genius counts. Teach and cultivate empathy and compassion for those who appear different. This will lead to respecting others and the unique sacred journey that each of us are on.

I challenge our teachers who are frustrated by what they see and their perceived inability to teach, and who have a desire to impact the children in their classroom to reframe how they see every child. Change begins with the smallest of steps; moving forward instead of being stuck in the old status quo is of utmost importance. When creating a beautiful painting, the entire canvas is not painted at the same time. You have to start with one color and one small area, and eventually the entire landscape will be completed. The world will be able to see the beauty of the whole, but it has to start with baby steps. You, our teachers, have such a huge role to play in humanity's evolution. Know that you do make a difference, no matter how small. Don't get swallowed up by the corporate giant of our educational system. You do matter, and you do have the power to model and teach cooperation within your classroom.

Taking the competitive paradigm out of our schools and replacing it with a new paradigm that emphasizes cooperation will honor our children for who they are, will allow for more children to feel and be successful, and will set an example of a new model for society that honors compassion and empathy toward others. We just have to remember, one step at a time, and never give up on our children. They need you.

Key Messages: Unwrapping Schools

» Children today thrive in an environment based on cooperation, because it feeds their empathic heart and their need to feel in harmony with others.

» Competition within our schools trickles down from administration to our teachers and ultimately to our students.

» Our schools are failing our kids, not the other way around.

» The world needs more individuals who are kind, creative, and sensitive to the needs of others.

» A child should be taught from the inside out, not just from the outside in.

» Waldorf School and The Project Approach are educational models that take the whole child approach to learning.

» Peace Literacy educates children about the basic inner needs of belonging and human behavior.

» Don't give up on a child just because their genius does not look like everyone else's.

» You can start in the classroom by modeling cooperation.

» Adopt an educational model that teaches compassion and empathy, such as the Peace Literacy model.

» Teach inner competition instead of outer competition.

PART III

*The Rise of Highly Sensitive
And Empathic Children*

CHAPTER 8

Unwrapping Empathy

*Understanding the rise of empaths and the
new age of consciousness*

Today's children and youth are showing us that humanity is making a shift from a strong external perception of events and circumstances to a more centered and balanced inner perception. They feel things more deeply than ever before, and this is why it is essential that we truly understand, respect, and honor the new and improved sensory sensitive child. For years, I have heard parents tell me stories of how they believe their child is reading their mind or that their child is picking up on the feelings and emotions of those around them. Many of these children have been described as overly sensitive and extremely compassionate toward others, often displaying behaviors such as anxiety, overwhelm, and shyness. I have heard stories about children of all ages, including babies and toddlers, showing their parents and even teachers true empathy, even when the adult is trying to hide their feelings. Emotion, like everything else, is simply energy that goes out into the world. We are moving towards a more empathic society, and this is evident today in the evolution of our children.

Energy and Healing the Empathic Heart

Everything is a form of energy. Our ears are able to pick up acoustical energy by converting it to mechanical energy in the eardrum and ossicular chain. Then, it is converted to hydraulic energy by the fluid-filled inner ear, then chemical energy at the level of the hair cell, and then electrical energy at the level of the brain. Eventually, the sound reaches the brain where it is heard, organized, and interpreted. We can't see sound, yet we are able to perceive it through a very complex auditory processing system. Our inner sensory processing system is capable of picking up and processing many other forms of energy that our physical body is not able to process. For example, mother's intuition is the internal knowing that something is wrong with her child. Or maybe you have had the experience when you know someone is about to call you, that something bad or good is about to happen, or that someone is watching you. We all have experienced the sense that there is more than meets the eye. Could it be possible that, through evolution, we are coming into this world more connected on a level that will allow us to develop more of our sensory system, particularly, our inner sensory system?

Scientists have been telling us for years that our brain is capable of so much more than what we are using now. So maybe it is possible that developing a stronger connection with our inner guidance system is where we are headed as a species. Accepting this as a possibility can help us to truly begin to help our children. When we accept and understand that they may be perceiving things differently and that this may be a positive evolutionary change, then we can help them first by not making them feel as if there is something wrong with them. By honoring who they are as part of the new normal, we will help them see themselves differently.

It is important to understand that since so many of our children may be sensing and feeling things on a deeper emotional level, then perhaps they are also picking up your feelings of worry and concern about them. When you look at your child and see their challenges or their disability as who they are, then you are not seeing them for their gifts and who they are at their core. When you see and focus on what you are perceiving as what is wrong with them, that is what they will internalize on an even deeper level than ever before. To put this in another way, when an individual has a higher sensitivity with their inner senses, then they are able to feel on an energetic level what the people around them are feeling and will quite often internalize those feelings. So, if those around them are constantly focusing on their weaknesses, then this is what they will perceive of themselves. However, if the people around them spend more time focusing on their strengths and their true awesomeness, then this is what they will feel and believe about themselves. Spending more time with loving, positive-based thoughts rather than fear-based thoughts will have a dramatic effect on how any child sees themselves and will create a true sense of belonging, value, and worthiness.

Here is an exercise that anyone can use and can be easily taught to a child. It's called, "What Would My Heart Say?" The purpose of this exercise is to build your empathy "muscle." It can be used anytime one is feeling stressed, hurt, angry, or any other negative emotion. Energy is running through us at every moment, and it can be fear-based or love-based. Note that this energy is different from the emotions of fear and love. For example, you can feel fear but still allow the energy of love to flow through and love the fear. This can be done throughout the day in order to build up the habit of allowing the flow of positive love energy, but it can also be used as an exercise with a child to help them connect with their heart and build on their natural tendency toward empathy and compassion.

Step 1) Set time aside to talk with your child about each other's days. It is important for your child to see you modeling this behavior and is a good way to get the exercise started, since your child may have difficulty at first coming up with an example. The goal is to discuss a particular situation from the day (an interaction with a friend, an event on the news, something that happened at school or work) and then ask a series of questions.

Step 2) Once you have discussed a particular situation, you now start with the questions.

a. *What would my heart say?* Encourage your child to become one of the characters in the situation and ask them what they would say if it was their heart talking. Have them tell you something that their heart is feeling while listening to the story and what their heart would want the people in the story to hear. You can point out how listening is not just done with the ears but is also done with the heart.

b. *What would my heart see?* Talk about what one would see if they were looking at the situation through the lens of their heart. Again, model this by adding some of your own ideas. This will help them see that there is more than meets the eye. Looking at something with your heart shines a different light on what is truly occurring.

c. *What would my heart do?* Maybe the story would have a different ending if something was done differently. Give examples of what your heart could do to help the people in the story and encourage your child to give examples as well. This will open the door to how things can have a different outcome when we follow the messages that come from our heart.

d. *What would my heart know?* Finally, you want to talk about anything that could be seen from the perspective of the heart that would help you and your child know something now that you were not aware of before. Summarize the story and the possible lesson that the heart wants you to know.

This is a beautiful exercise to do that both you and your child will benefit from. If your family works with a speech therapist or teacher, consider sharing it with them. It is a great exercise to do in a group, since everyone can benefit from the different perspectives that each child may have. For instance, the teacher can present the story and then the class can participate in answering and discussing the different questions.

Benefits:

- Helps children to cultivate and develop their natural-born attribute of empathy.

- Encourages creativity and imagination.

- Builds on listening skills and helps children to learn empathy through listening and giving their attention to others.

- Gives the teacher the opportunity to show children how there are different perspectives to the same situation and how our own experiences in life shape what we see.

- Demonstrates how we all have a choice in what we do at any given time and in any situation.

- Helps in strengthening their internal guidance system and encourages them to trust their inner knowing.

- Provides an opportunity to discuss the importance of taking care of themselves and how they can protect their own energy by maintaining a strong connection with their heart.

Inner Versus Physical Hearing

As an audiologist who has studied many types of auditory deprivation, I have seen many highly sensitive children and have started to see patterns in the advantages of sensitivity. One of those advantages is related to inner listening. There are two types of listening: external and internal. External listening is done with the ears and the entire auditory processing system. As an individual connects to the physical presence of sound in their physical environment, their physical ears begin to map and make sense of the sounds around them. They become more and more auditorily engaged and therefore develop a strong and healthy auditory processing system. With consistent engagement, their auditory system will continue to develop stronger and faster connections. Internal listening, on the other hand, does not require the use of the physical ear. In fact, listening with the physical ear may be a form of distraction that, over time, may cause inner listening deprivation, and in turn can cause a person to disconnect from their internal listening, or guidance system.

A friend of mine who also happens to be a high-profile psychic medium once told me that his family thought there was something wrong with him, because he didn't seem to be hearing and developed speech and language skills later than normal. He was often accused of not listening, and there were concerns about his actual hearing. His hearing was fine; he just did not have to listen to anyone, because he knew what they were going to say before they would actually say it. He found noise very distracting and wanted to tune it all out so that he could listen without his ears. He was tuning in to his internal listening system and was able to develop and maintain a strong connection to his inner guidance system. Today, he continues to receive messages by using his inner listening skills and is making a pretty good living helping people receive messages that they are not able to hear themselves. His story made me wonder whether sensitive children "tune out" external noise on purpose, so they can better "tune in" to their internal listening systems.

It's possible that many more of our children today are being born with this extra sensitive sense of inner hearing, and it could account for some of the increase in the diagnoses of auditory processing delays and speech and language delays. Maybe this is why so many parents have reported to me throughout the years that their child seemed to have good hearing and appeared to understand everything they said, but as they grew older and language became more abstract, they seemed to have more difficulty processing language, and therefore, processing auditory information as well. If this is true, then we could help a child connect their physical listening system without losing the connection with their inner listening system. What if we were able to help these children find balance in developing both the internal and external processing systems? Perhaps this is where we are headed in humanity's evolutionary process.

The Dark Side of Empathy

Around age two, most children begin forming their sense of self or their unique individual ego. This is when children begin to see themselves as separate from those around them. By the age of seven, the average child has pretty much formed their own unique sense of who they are, complete with a belief system that can include both positive and negative beliefs about themselves. A child's experiences within that first seven years is very important in the shaping and molding of their own ego. Children who have experienced mostly failure during that time will think of themselves as a failure. Those who have experienced mostly success during this important time period will think of themselves as successful. Typically, external circumstances play a very important role in the developing of the ego mind. This would also fall under the category of external intellect, or knowledge.

However, a child who has a very strong internal intellect, or a strong sense of knowing what an extraordinary person they are, may become very conflicted over time if they are not encouraged to develop this inner sense. If they are consistently met with external circumstances that don't fit their inner knowing, they will become increasingly confused and frustrated by what they are feeling. When the external and the internal are on opposite sides of the spectrum, it can result in a lot of mind chatter. They might feel smart and stupid at the same time. A constant battle is going on inside between the inner knowing and the external belief system, and the louder voice is the one that will win out.

In some cases, the louder voice will be the inner knowing. Usually in this case, it is because there has been enough external evidence to tip the scale and allow the inner voice to be heard by softening the outer voice. However, when the outer voice continues to be fed with outside circumstances reinforcing its false belief system and the inner voice that started out being a strength slowly becomes silent, this is a recipe for disaster. This scenario can cause a huge egoic battle within, resulting in a person completely losing touch with who they are. The egoic mind is continuing to look for outside circumstances to prove their inner knowing of their value and importance in this world, but instead, it is constantly listening to the voice coming from their external intellect and programming, which is in direct opposition with their inner knowing. The external messages need to reinforce the internal knowing. If there is a mismatch between these two sources of identity, the result for a sensitive child can be devastating, especially in the face of negative events.

What happens when the sensitive child's beautiful gifts are not cultivated and developed, and they experience multiple negative experiences? Many children are born into violent homes or abusive situations, are picked on and bullied, and are faced with challenges in school both educationally and socially. Although these situations are extremely unfortunate and no child should have to endure these types of hardships, why is it that some of these children eventually make it out of these negative environments and others never do? Why is it that today so many children are turning to drugs and alcohol at such a young age? What causes a child to want to hurt others or even themselves? What causes a child to snap and eventually commit horrendous acts of violence? There are many external factors that we can contribute to this, from violence in video games and on TV to domestic violence and access to violent messages online. As a society, it is natural that we would want to look toward outside influences to explain these behaviors. However, I believe we are missing a very important element here and want to propose that sensitivity is a beautiful attribute that more and more of our children are being born with today, but heightened sensitivity also leaves children more vulnerable in the face of repeated negative experiences.

Children who are extra sensitive feel things much more deeply and process information such as feelings and emotions on a very deep level. When this trait is cultivated and developed, these children are compassionate and empathic toward others. When this trait is not nurtured or understood, a child will seek ways to protect themselves from their overpowering feelings. They will create beliefs about themselves, the people in their life, and the world they live in. Many extra sensitive individuals turn to the use of drugs and alcohol in order to numb the overpowering feelings that they do not understand. When they endure repeated trauma, they have to develop ways to protect themselves from the deep feelings of shame, guilt, worthlessness, and lack of belonging. In some cases, these children are successful in shutting down their feelings, which can appear as aloofness, lack of motivation, shyness, and in extreme cases narcissistic behavior. However, I believe that many of the children today who are committing horrific acts, such as the many school shootings that are happening today, are children who started out extra sensitive, but repeated traumas compounded by added stimulation of violence from external sources, converted their empathy into something darker. These children feel that they have no other option. They reached the tipping point that causes their beautiful empathic heart to go into hiding and to choose narcissism over empathy. Their pain is felt so deeply that protection mode kicks in and unfortunate choices are made. This can explain why there are so many children turning to drugs and alcohol, why the suicide rate has significantly increased among our young people, and why there are so many school shootings happening today.

I truly believe that our tendency to ignore and neglect our sensory sensitive children is one of the reasons for so many school shootings today. Many of these shooters have a history of diagnoses such as autism and Asperger's. Adam Lanza, who was responsible for the Sandy Hook Elementary School shooting on December 14, 2012, was reported as having Asperger's syndrome, a form of autism. Nikolas Cruz, who was responsible for the Stoneman Douglas High School shooting on February 14, 2018, was reported as having autism. It is common with these diagnoses that the physical senses have difficulty organizing and making sense out of the information they are receiving. When these children are placed in educational settings that do not teach to their strengths, or where they are bored and don't feel challenged, the inner conflict begins with the added struggle of feeling emotions such as shame and unworthiness on such a deep level without understanding and support. If you mix this with a social experience that makes them feel different and devalued, then you are headed in the direction of inner turmoil that can have very damaging effects. Their inner knowing of who they are is not being supported by their external circumstances. Their experiences mislead them into believing that they are someone they are not, and as a desperate act to try to fit in, they begin trying on different masks in order to feel accepted. But these masks are not real and, for some, may feel quite uncomfortable. And as often is the case, the masks quite simply do not work. These children are left feeling more and more out of place, putting a big target on their back for possible bullying and misunderstanding.

With every negative experience, that voice in the head that was born out of previous negative experiences just gets louder and louder. The inner knowing fights to hold on, but the false beliefs and repetitive negative experiences are too much to handle, especially by someone who is already exceptionally sensitive and has a history of social emotional challenges. Feeling different, alone, and as though no one understands or even cares can wreak havoc inside a person's mind. This is what is happening today. Highly sensitive individuals are being bombarded by so much external stimuli that is radically out of alignment with who they are at their core that they eventually snap and commit horrific crimes in their desperate plea for help in a world that has created so much internal pain. They have not been given the appropriate tools necessary to understand their own unique operating system, and to make it worse they have been placed in the harshest environments that have continually and repeatedly fed their computer with trash that goes against their true nature. Eventually, their operating system has no option but to crash. If school is the place where much of the trash programming is being installed, then it helps to explain why so many of these tragic events are occurring right now. There are many people talking about what should be done to stop this problem, such as gun control and anti-bullying awareness campaigns, but I truly believe that in order to really stop these events from occurring, we truly need to change our educational paradigm from one of competition to one of cooperation.

Let's look at this a little more closely. If a child wears the label of autism spectrum disorder or Asperger's syndrome, then we look at them through the lens of these disorders, and we attempt to educate them within a certain framework. We recognize that they have difficulty processing their surroundings through their physical senses, so we give them therapies and provide behavior modification programs in order to shape and mold them into behaving as close to a "normal" child as possible. However, if they have an extra sensitive inner sensory processing system, then they feel things on a much deeper level. If they are not feeling loved and accepted for who they are, then they will feel as if there is something wrong with them. These feelings will grow and develop into feelings of being devalued and worthless. Many children grow up with feelings of not fitting in and of not being loved or accepted, but what causes a child to snap and commit such horrendous acts? I believe the answers lie in the depth of their feelings and their experiences.

I believe that these children start out loving, but there is a constant battle brewing inside of them that is trying to feel good but is attached to external circumstances that are conflicting with their inner knowing. Eventually, the voices from the external world that are saying they are worthless, broken, and no good become so loud that they forget who they are at their core. They are desperate to be seen and heard. All they want is to be accepted for who they are, but they can't stop the deep feelings of helplessness from taking over. Children with positive, loving experiences growing up will be more likely to become positive, caring members of society with an inner desire to be of service to others. However, the other end of the spectrum is possible if these children grow up with extreme negative experiences.

I just can't stress this enough. I truly believe this is a tragedy that does not have to occur if we can begin to look at our children with loving eyes and support them by honoring their authenticity and their unique gifts. Every child unwrapped is about giving every child the opportunity to be happy in their own skin and celebrating the awesomeness that lives within each of us without feeling the need to change, shape, and mold. We may not be able to protect every child from traumatic events, but we can educate them and give them the tools they need to make positive choices. We can help them to understand and develop their empathy instead of fearing it and being ashamed of it.

We need to value and honor every child for their unique gifts.

We need a learning environment that teaches to every child's strengths and rewards them for being the beautiful souls they are here to be.

We need a society that sees the value and worthiness in every human being no matter their age, gender, race, intellect, or neurodiversity.

We need more individuals who have the
inner strength of knowing with a high level of
sensitivity and loving kindness toward others.

We need to cultivate and develop the inner gift
of empathy with which each one of us is born.

We need to help children understand why
people adopt certain behaviors and help them
to make choices from the heart.

The youth today do have a strong knowing, and they are not afraid to follow their heart even if it goes against old societal beliefs. Helping them develop these strengths is something we can do as parents, as educators, and as a society.

The Power of a Positive Environment

Using Dr. Judith Orloff's distinction between highly sensitive people and empaths, we will take a closer look at the unique experiences of an empathic child. Let's consider for a moment how an empathic child experiences childhood development. A child who is empathic is connecting to the physical world through their physical senses yet at the same time remains strongly connected to their inner senses and the metaphysical world. Growing up as an empath can be very challenging both for the child and the parent of an empathic child. Understanding this "perfect storm" can make things much easier for all concerned. Consider that, not only is this child being bombarded by physical experiences that they have to sort and make sense out of, but they also have to sort through all the emotional and energetic muck that surrounds them.

At age eight, Brittany is extremely empathic. She was also slow to develop speech and language, is somewhat uncoordinated, and is very shy around new people and new situations. Her mother has been bringing her to different therapists and doctors since she was three years old, and now in the third grade she is really struggling in school. Brittany's mom has been fighting with the school district now for two years and often finds herself very frustrated with the lack of support and understanding that she is receiving from the school. Having her daughter now in the third grade, Brittany's mom is very upset with Brittany's teacher, because she feels her teacher just does not understand Brittany. Mom knows that Brittany is really smart, but she just doesn't understand why she is struggling so much in school. And if that wasn't enough, now Brittany is starting to have trouble socially. For mom, this is just another area of frustration that is keeping her up at night. Mom is concerned that her daughter is not going to be able to develop strong friendships and fears that she will be made fun of, which will further destroy her self-confidence.

Let's take a deeper look into what Brittany may be experiencing. She goes to school every day where she compares herself to other children. She sees the other children learning in school, yet she struggles to learn. She often gets pulled out of her class for extra help that the other children don't seem to need. Her homework seems to take forever, and she just doesn't understand why she has such a hard time learning the things that the other children seem to learn easily. The other children never seem to want to play with her. She tries to engage with them, but she often feels overwhelmed and shuts down. She doesn't think they like her. She just feels different. At home, Brittany senses her mother's frustration. Brittany knows that her frustration is due to her struggle with learning. Brittany does not like being the source of her mother's pain. It hurts her to know that her mother is suffering so much, because she is not smart. She actually feels her mother's pain, and she feels as if it is all her fault. Brittany tries harder and harder, yet she still comes up short. Soon, Brittany starts displaying fears and anxieties. When she goes to school, she often complains of headaches or stomachaches. She shuts down more and more, which further concerns her mother.

In response to this concern, mom seeks out advice from Brittany's pediatrician, who refers her out to have a neuropsychological assessment that in turn leads to a diagnosis of "social anxiety disorder." With this diagnosis, Brittany is given a series of medications in order to help her cope with her anxieties. Over the course of two years, Brittany's doctor raises her medication dose three times due to increased stress and anxiety. Now, Brittany is 10 years old, and whenever her anxieties are at a heightened level, she asks her mom if she can get an increase in her medication dosage. Brittany believes the medication is helping her, and she has learned to rely on it. However, the medication is only treating the symptoms and not the underlying cause. The cause of her anxieties is not that she is having trouble sorting out all of the mixed signals that she is receiving; rather, she does not understand how she is feeling and that these feelings make her feel different, and therefore she feels there must be something wrong with her. She is overwhelmed by what she is feeling, and she does not know how to feel better.

Now, let's look at this in a different way. What if instead of feeling as if there was something wrong with her, Brittany was taught that not only was there nothing wrong with her, but in fact her sensitivities were actually her gifts? With the proper understanding and acceptance of her beautiful perfection, Brittany could learn ways to protect her emotions and thrive in this world. She could grow up loving the perfection of who she is instead of being ashamed of the perception of imperfection.

I believe that many of these children also have difficulty connecting to their physical world through their physical sensory processing system. When a child is born, they are immediately bombarded by physical stimuli. The central nervous system in turn begins organizing this information in order to make sense of this physical world. Our physical senses connect us to our physical world. As we become more connected with our physical world, we become less connected with our metaphysical world or our inner world. However, if a child comes into this world with a heightened inner processing system, then it may be more difficult for them to wire and connect with the density of the physical world and remain more connected with the metaphysical world, their divinity. They feel things more deeply, so they will feel fear more deeply and therefore be more susceptible to anxieties. An empath can also feel pain and emotions that are not theirs and can become easily overwhelmed by all the different energies around them.

For some, the word empath may be frightening, but we are all capable of empathy. For some people, however, that switch is turned to high all the time. It is difficult to turn it off, because it is their natural state. Imagine for a moment what it would be like if for one day you felt all the emotions of the people around you. You are bombarded by emotions such as anger, fear, sadness, and frustration. You may also feel the positive emotions of others such as joy, love, hope, and happiness. Everywhere you go, you feel these emotions from others. When an individual is exposed to so many different emotions of others, it can make it extremely difficult to sort out their own emotions. This generally would lead to their own emotions being that of confusion, apprehensiveness, and anxiety. Not understanding the source of this anxiety can lead a person to want to withdraw from people and spend more time alone, which in turn may lead to being labeled as having social anxiety disorder. Since we want to treat disorders in this country with pharmaceuticals, many of these children end up on anti-anxiety medications, anti-depressants, and other anti-this and anti-that medications.

It is also quite common for many of these children to be the target of bullying. In the past, these children have represented a smaller portion of our population; however, I believe many more of our children are being born with this beautiful gift.

Here is an idea. What if these children are here to save the world. What would that feel like? These children have a stronger connection with their heart. I can think of many brilliant people who would benefit from being a little more connected with their hearts, such as doctors, lawyers, and politicians, just to name a few. Being more connected with our hearts can allow us to see the world in a more beautiful way. When understood, welcomed, and treated as the beautiful gift it is, it will lead to positive emotions such as joy, peace, bliss, confidence, and love. When these children are placed in a positive nurturing environment, where they are free to be who they are and are led to understand what a beautiful gift their sensitivity is, then they will feel these positive emotions very deeply instead. When this gift is misunderstood, however, it can cause fear, and fear leads to negative emotions, such as cynicism, anger, mistrust, hurtfulness, sadness, and confusion. We label our children as sensory seeking and sensory sensitive, but what if what we are really seeing is a shift to developing a stronger inner guidance system?

Children today feel things on a deeper level than ever before. Even children who don't seem to be in touch with their emotions might really be so overwhelmed by all the stimuli around them that they have to shut down in order to feel safe. Many parents have repeatedly witnessed meltdowns due to sensory overload and look at external sources as the culprit. But how about sensory overload on an emotional level, such as when a child is not able to regulate their emotions or when there just doesn't seem to be any external cause for their meltdown? Many parents also report that their sensitive children seem to be "out of sorts" when events such as natural and man-made disasters occur around the world. I have heard from many parents talk about how their children react with true empathy and sadness in response to tragic events that are happening around the world, even when they have not been told about the event. Teachers have also reported that they notice a change in their students during and after traumatic events that have not directly affected them. With this heightened inner guidance system, our youth today are feeling things more deeply. They have a stronger sense of knowing what is right and what is wrong and have a stronger sense within themselves that allows them to differentiate between what feels good and what does not feel good. This inner guidance system, when developed and trusted, is a truly beautiful gift to have, but it needs to be cultivated and developed.

New Age of Consciousness

"No problem can be solved from the same level of consciousness that created it."
—Albert Einstein

Let's consider for a moment that "what if" more children today are being born with a heightened metaphysical sensory system due to evolution and are therefore having more difficulty connecting and organizing their physical senses? Is it possible that this is the beginning of the new norm? This would explain why more children today are being diagnosed with learning disabilities and developmental delays than ever before. It could also help explain why we have more and more children and youth on anti-anxiety medications today, why alcohol and drug addiction, suicide, and self-injury are on the rise with our youth, and why we have more and more tragic school shootings happening around this country.

In the book *A Whole New Mind,* Daniel Pink describes what he refers to as the move into the "Conceptual Age." From the Agricultural Age that consisted of farmers, to the Industrial Age that consisted of factory workers, to the Informational Age that consisted of thinkers and knowledge workers, we are now moving into the Conceptual Age or the Age of Consciousness, which consists of creators and empathizers. Pink points out that the right-brain qualities of creativity and empathy are greatly on the rise and that many of the jobs held by left-brain thinkers are being replaced by computers, just as many jobs once held by manual laborers were replaced by machines in the late 19th century. Today and going forward, those who can problem solve, create, and show true empathy toward others will be our leaders. One good example of this would be Ryan Levesque, creator of the "Ask Method." Using empathy and his understanding of marketing, Ryan created this program in which he teaches entrepreneurs how to market and build their business by asking people what it is that they truly want. He points out that if you take the time to ask people what they are feeling and what they are struggling with, then you will be able to understand them on a deeper level, which will help you to create solutions to help solve their biggest frustrations and problems. Ryan created a multimillion-dollar business just by teaching people what to ask, how to listen, and why empathy is vitally important when it comes to the future of business.

When we look back in history, we see how humanity has evolved. With every generation, we seem to be one step closer in the evolutionary process of humanitarianism. From such things as slavery, labor conditions, criminal punishments, prison reform, and racial cleansing, we are making strides in a more compassionate direction, even if it may not always seem like it. Is it possible that this new generation of empathic children are the evolutionary gifts to the world? If so, then maybe we should start looking at them through different eyes and start honoring their gifts instead of labeling their differences. Can you imagine a world where everyone has an inner guidance system that would point them in the right direction to what was of the highest good for all? That ability paired with a society based on cooperation instead of competition would insure a more peaceful and compassionate world. This is where we are headed, but to get there, we have to travel through some very turbulent times, which is often the case with change. We also need to understand this change so that we can help our children be better equipped to lead us down this new path. Understanding and then honoring these beautiful gifts, regardless of the outside wrapping, will enable our children to grow and develop into the extraordinary individuals each of us were meant to be.

What we can learn from our children is that, by looking beyond the physical and into the inner light that shines within each of us, we will be guided out of the darkness and into a more beautiful and compassionate world. The old paradigm is one that looks to external circumstances for guidance and direction. We look at history to guide us into the future by focusing on external events. The new paradigm is one in which we look within for new answers. We can't keep heading in the old direction. Things have to change in order to survive. We have to continue to evolve as we have been doing for centuries, and evolution is leading us on a path inward. As individuals, we are all on a journey of self-discovery.

Today, more and more people are discovering that by slowing down and quieting the mind, they are able to become more peaceful and self-aware. We are looking at our experiences as a way to grow and develop inside. In developing a strong external connection through our physical senses with the physical world around us, we have lost touch with our inner senses that connect us to the world within and to each other. The movement toward self-discovery is helping so many of us to get back in touch with who we truly are at our core, the beauty that lies within each and every one of us. Our attachment to external circumstances has caused us to forget this. We have been wearing so many masks throughout our lifetime, trying to fit in and follow the status quo, that we have forgotten who we are. At a certain point in our lives, we make the decision to get back in touch with our true essence and find ourselves and our path.

For far too long, humanity has been out of balance, relying more on the external senses than on their inner senses. However, this is all changing thanks to evolution and the need mankind has right now to bring more compassion into the world. Our children are answering this desperate call to bring more balance to the world. Parents today play a very important role in helping our children grow and developing a more harmonious and balanced relationship to the world and to each other. Our education system must also change and adapt in order to assure that youth are truly seen and heard for the messages that they are here to deliver. Helping move this process along begins with understanding and accepting what is happening, so that we can stop hindering our children's ability to share their gifts and start helping them expand and grow their gifts. It starts by taking the time to look beyond what we have come to know as reality and start to see a new reality where every child is seen for their unique awesomeness and every child's gifts are unwrapped in order for the world to see with new eyes. The time has arrived for us to help our children balance all of their senses, to learn from our youth, and to rediscover our own awesomeness and our own inner strengths.

Key Messages: Unwrapping Empathy

» Is there a tipping point where an empathic heart turns narcissistic in order to protect itself from deep feelings of shame?

» Everything is a form of energy.

» It is important to find balance and harmony between the inner and outer senses.

» Children need to be given the tools that they need in order to understand their own unique processing system.

» Children need a learning environment that teaches to their unique strengths and honors their diversity.

» Empathy needs to be cultivated and developed.

» There are unique challenges that empathic children and their parents face.

» When a child comes into this world with a heightened inner sensory system, it may be more difficult for them to develop and connect to the physical world through their physical senses.

» When an empathic child is exposed to many different emotions of others, it may be difficult for them to sort out their own emotions.

» There are many brilliant people who could benefit from being a little more connected to their heart energy, such as doctors, lawyers, and politicians.

» By looking beyond the physical and into the inner light that shines within each of us, we will be guided out of the darkness and into a more beautiful and compassionate world.

» The new paradigm is one in which we look within for answers and guidance.

» For far too long, man has been out of balance, relying more on the external senses than on their inner senses.

CHAPTER 9

Unwrapping Purpose

*Understanding each person's purpose and how
we can follow our children into a beautiful
tomorrow*

I often hear parents tell me that everyone should spend a day sitting in my waiting room so that they could see that their own challenges were not so bad. I remember watching my brother struggle in school as a child and later as an adult trying to find his way and witnessing my mother's stress in trying to understand and ultimately help her son. The suffering of these two people in my life has ignited in me an unending desire to find the answers to my questions and the questions of so many people who have been struggling to feel good about who they are. For years, I thought the answer was to help as many children as I could and to support the many parents out there searching for answers. When I started writing this book, that was my goal. But now I see that the answer goes way beyond helping parents understand their children. After all, most parents have an inner knowing of how awesome their children are. However, they are also faced with fighting their inner knowing with their societal belief system that keeps them in fear and fight mode, trying to defend and ultimately help their children thrive in a world that is stuck in an old paradigm that no longer serves our children of today. One of the biggest concerns I hear from parents is that of how their child is perceived by others. They worry about how they will be treated by their peers and by society in general. It is my ultimate hope and desire that this book serves as a catalyst to the change that our children desperately need. It is time that the education system and all the administrators and politicians who are responsible for our children's education finally wake up and realize the importance and value of every child today, regardless of their unique packaging.

A Lesson from Mother Nature

Recently, I had the exciting opportunity to visit South Africa with my daughter. It was a beautiful trip, and one of the highlights was an African safari, getting up close and personal with so many animals living in their own habitat. Our guide was so very passionate about sharing his heart and love for the animals with all of us and was filled with fascinating information, including the importance of rhinoceros dung. You see, rhino dung attracts a great variety of animals and insects, such as dung flies and dung beetles, as well as lizards and a variety of birds that feed on the insects. The chemicals in a rhino's poop can communicate to other rhinos information such as sex, age, general health, and reproductive status. In fact, every living element plays an important role in the ecosystem, from the giant elephants and rhinos, to the insects, plants and yes, even the poop. Without the rhinos, which they predict may be extinct very soon due to the illegal poaching, there would be no rhino dung, and it would only be a matter of time before many species of insects and the animals that feed on those insects, would also become extinct.

In Marianne Williamson's book *Tears to Triumph*, she tells a story of a group of anthropologists who come across a troop of chimpanzees and notice depressed behavior among some of the chimps. The anthropologists decided to remove the depressed chimps, and when they returned later to observe the original group, they were surprised to find that they had all died. It seemed the chimps with depressed behavior served a purpose within the group, potentially by warning the other chimps about possible danger. Without their presence in the group, the rest of the chimps were not able to survive. This story, along with the importance of everything within the ecosystem having value, demonstrates the importance of everyone. No matter how large or small, strong or weak, outgoing or shy, everyone plays an important role in society.

On our African safari, we also learned about how trees communicate with one another and with animals. Trees release a chemical that will reach the leaves and cause them to become very bitter. This chemical release occurs after a giraffe has been eating the leaves for a period of time, and the bitter taste keeps the giraffe from staying in one place and eating up all the leaves on one tree, ultimately wiping it out as a supportive food source. The trees also communicate with each other by sending out a message to the trees that are downwind, so they can start to prepare for their chemicals to be released. This also assures that the herds of giraffes follow a particular route while they spend the majority of the day feeding.

This experience stood out to me for two reasons. First, it demonstrates how communication in nature is not dependent on the physical senses, and yet, there is so much communication going on every moment that is essential to the survival of our ecosystem. If trees and animals can communicate energetically, then it shouldn't be hard to believe that we can as well. It's just that the inner communication gets drowned out by the external communication system as our physical hearing develops. Second, it reinforces the importance of every living thing in nature. Every element plays an important role and is equally important, no matter how large or how small. In our society, I believe this is also true. Everything and everyone serves a very important role that is necessary for our survival. As humanity evolves, our biology adapts in order to ensure the survival of our species.

We have been told for years that our brain is capable of so much more than what we are presently using. What if humanity is adapting what it needs in order to develop a more harmonious and balanced society based on cooperation? If this were the case, then it may be quite helpful to have more children who are born with the ability to sense, feel, and create and who have a strong connection with their inner self and their sense of knowing. It is also quite possible that, at least in some cases, children may have a little more difficulty connecting and organizing their physical senses. They may appear more sensitive and empathetic than they have in the past and may have different learning needs. Unfortunately, we live in a world today in which we disregard many different populations of people, such as our elderly and our individuals with developmental delays.

The Need for More Understanding

In 1992, I decided to expand my practice and began seeing a large population of patients who were diagnosed with autism. I needed a larger office, so I made the move into an office building. I was surprised to find that other people in the building complained daily about this new population of people who were coming into the building. They mainly complained to the superintendent of the building, who would then report to me that people were uncomfortable riding in the elevator or sharing the public restroom with my clients. Instead of coming to me to learn more about them so that perhaps they could be more accepting and less threatened by them, they just continued to complain to the building management and make requests that I vacate the building. I will say that not everyone felt that way, and over time, many of them became more accepting of my "different" clientele, but there were still those who complained throughout my stay there. Eventually, I bought a house in which I was able to convert the downstairs into an office. The house was zoned for commercial use, but still I received complaints in the beginning about my "special" clientele. Lack of understanding and empathy for this population and their parents who were seeking help for their children led to many problems.

I recall one incident where a mother had parked in front of my neighbor's house (who happened to be the real estate agent who originally sold me the house and assured me that parking would not be an issue). My neighbor and her husband were sitting on their front lawn, and when the mom got out of her car with her two sons, one of whom was autistic, the couple asked her to move the car. The mother asked if she could move it later, but they insisted that she move it right away. So she had to climb back into her car with her son who became very confused about why they were getting back into the car and had a major meltdown, kicking and screaming. Sadly, my neighbors just sat there and watched the incident, never offering to let the mom leave her car there. By the time the mom and her son had come into my office, they were both physically and emotionally exhausted.

Recently, I heard from a mother who had brought her son to me when he was 14 years old. He was in his 30s now, and she was looking for treatment for her son who had suffered a traumatic brain injury. As a child, he was diagnosed as having autism, but over time, he developed verbal skills and was able to communicate. After the accident, his skills started to decline, and the mom was hoping that the treatments that had worked for him as a child might work again. During our conversation, the mom shared with me the tragic story of how the traumatic brain injury happened. Her son was living in a building in New York City, and for the most part people in the building were accepting of him and loved him. However, over time the building management changed, and many new residents moved in. This young man grew up and was now an adult living at home with his mother who cared for him. He was often picked on by the other residents, and the problems were gradually getting worse. One day, he became overwhelmed and had a meltdown. The residents became nervous and called the police. When the police tried to escort him away from the area, he had another meltdown and resisted the police, since he did not like being touched or restrained. The police used a Taser on him, and after a series of other events, some of which are not clear, he ended up with a traumatic brain injury and spent several months in jail. When his mom called me, he was living in a residential setting three hours away and was not allowed back in his home. Lack of understanding and acceptance of this young man led to this very sad situation.

In today's world, we are very quick to disregard not only people with disabilities we don't understand, but we are also quick to dismiss our elderly population. With the rapid growth of this population, we are often faced with how to care for so many people who are in need of assistance. Not everyone is able to or even wants to live with family members who can be their caretakers, which leaves us with the need for facilities that can adequately care for this population. The problem that many people may not be aware of is that these facilities are quickly becoming a huge business. They can be quite profitable, and many companies are investing in this rapidly growing business. Unfortunately, as often happens in business, profit is treated as a higher priority than people. I have personally experienced this with my father when he reached the point in his life where he needed help caring for himself. After a year and a half of living in an assisted living residence, I received an early morning phone call letting me know that he had been brutally beat up in the middle of the night and had been taken to the hospital. My father passed away as a result of those injuries, as well as continued neglect after the assault. His death is a painful example of society's lack of care for this vulnerable population and its prioritization of business over people. In Texas, there is legislation in place that protects nursing homes, hospitals, and other facilities from being sued, which allows these businesses to operate with little risk of a potential lawsuit. It is also interesting to note that they are ranked 50th in the country for care and safety but ranked number one in profitability, clearly demonstrating the failure of this legislation. Many of the facilities in Texas are being built with fancy exteriors and plenty of bells and whistles that have the appearance of a wonderful facility. In reality, they are understaffed, and the little staff they do have lack the minimal experience necessary to fulfill many of the positions.

As a society, I don't believe we value these populations, and this is a tremendous shame. In our ecosystem, every person, animal, insect, plant, organism and yes, even rhino dung, has value. There is so much we can stand to learn from our elderly, from our so-called disabled, from our children and adults with autism and other developmental challenges. And there is certainly a lot we can learn from our beautifully sensitive children, no matter what type of package they come in. Everyone plays an essential role in society and with humanity. We are all in this together, and we are all part of the same whole. Sensitivity, empathy, and cooperation are all essential to our existence. We are evolving, and while we may be experiencing some tremendous growing pains at the moment, I believe we are headed to a more beautiful tomorrow. Our children are here to help lead the way.

Only Love Can Save Us Now

We all have dreams of what we want for our children. So, what happens when those dreams do not become reality? What happens when our experiences were not in our playbook and seem to have jumped off the page into a book we could never have imagined? What happens when hope fades away and is replaced with disappointment? The key here is empathy and learning to love what is. But, what is love? Most of us would answer this question by describing human love. But what is real love or true love? We have all heard the term unconditional love, and we know that this is truly a beautiful thing to experience. But what most of us experience day-to-day is human love. Most of us think of love as a feeling that then gets expressed with words and emotions. But what is the underlying principle of love? What is love at its core?

True love is an energy that holds this world together. It is who we are in our truest nature. It comes from our heart and is a constant. It is internal and eternal. It never changes, and it is not dependent on anything outside of us. Human love, on the other hand, comes from our mind and is dependent on outside circumstances and thoughts. For example, we meet someone who is wonderful and makes us feel in a way that we have associated with love. They make us feel loved by what they say, the things they do, and the kindness they show. Then one day, they do something or say something that does not feel good. We begin to experience negative feelings for that same person who used to bring us so much joy and love. Now, the thoughts that are associated with that person are ones of pain, anger, sadness, or hurt. We might even decide that we no longer love that person. This is an example of human love, because it comes from the mind and is based on feelings that come from our thoughts. Human love has an element of fear associated with it, but true love, or unconditional love, is just pure love.

Attachment to human love can lead to disappointment and feelings of unworthiness, shame, guilt, and low self-esteem. This is what happens when our experiences are not in alignment with our thoughts or what we think "should be." Thoughts such as, "This shouldn't be happening," "He/she shouldn't have done that," "I should have known better," or "They should have known better" are all thoughts that will quickly lead you right down the rabbit hole of disappointment, frustration, and overwhelm. Mind chatter is what pulls us away from the heart and feelings of love. Reframing our thoughts and our beliefs will lead us back to our heart by centering our feelings around loving thoughts. One of the biggest challenges many of us have faced growing up is learning to love ourselves. Learning to love ourselves comes from being comfortable with who we are. It also comes from feeling loved by those around us. When we genuinely feel loved by people who are important to us, such as our family, then we feel worthy of love. It is very hard to love yourself when you are constantly trying to fit in and do not feel comfortable being your authentic self. It is important to teach a sensitive child the difference between human love and true love, so that their heart energy can expand instead of contract.

According to Maslow's hierarchy of needs, feeling loved and a sense of belonging is the third essential need, following physiological needs (food, water, sleep) and the need to feel safe. He proposed that our basic needs are what motivate our behavior. If a particular need is not met, the motivation to fulfill that need will become stronger and stronger. If a child does not feel loved by those around them or doesn't feel a sense of belonging, they are more and more motivated to fulfill that need, even if it means wearing a mask and trying to change themselves in order to fit into the accepted model. Eventually, not fulfilling that need will lead to deep feelings of shame and unworthiness.

Maslow recognized that self-actualization was not only the goal in life but that it is actually our natural state. He wrote, "I think of the self-actualizing man not as an ordinary man with something added, but rather as the ordinary man with nothing taken away." In other words, our goal is to be our authentic self. We are all here to be exactly who we are, but different experiences will shape our world and cause us to perceive ourselves differently than who we truly are at our core. Within the hierarchy of needs model, we have both physical needs and inner needs. Our basic physical needs of food, clothing, and shelter need to be met to support us physiologically. Our need for safety includes both physical and emotional safety. Emotional safety is an inner need that goes beyond our physical needs and is essential to meeting our physical needs. In fact, our inner needs are just as important, if not more important, than our physical needs.

Maslow's hierarchy of needs is based on an old paradigm, where we look at the world through an outside-in perspective. When we look at our hierarchy of needs based on a new paradigm with an inside-out perspective of the world, we would see that our inner needs come first in order to assure our outer or physical needs are met. For example, an infants' purpose is to connect to the physical world by developing their sensory processing system. In the new paradigm, they are also developing and balancing their inner senses. Their inner need of purpose motivates their physical development, and their inner need to feel safe guides their play and their development. If a child does not feel safe in their physical world or in their body, then the course of physical development will be altered. When we teach Maslow's hierarchy of needs, we are placing emphasis on the external needs and supporting an outside-in view of the world. Shifting the importance of needs to an inside-out view of the world puts emphasis on an individual's inner needs of purpose, belonging, and sense of self. It teaches a child that they are important for who they are at their core and motivates them to develop their own unique gifts.

According to the Centers for Disease Control and Prevention, suicide rates among teens and young adults have nearly tripled since the 1940s. What is happening on the inside of our children to cause this tragedy? I believe it is time that we start spending more time educating ourselves and our children on the importance of developing our inner needs. If we create a new hierarchy of needs, then we will see that the elements associated with developing our inner needs, such as having a sense of purpose, a sense of belonging, a sense of value, and a sense of self, are all essential to life itself. These are all needs of the heart. Living a purposeful life starts with understanding and trusting our own unique guidance system or intuition. Yes, reading and writing are important, but what value does it have if you feel lost with no sense of purpose? Helping our children develop the skills necessary to create a life with a strong positive sense of purpose should be our most important goal. To begin with, we need to focus on helping them build a strong sense of worthiness. Children must feel as if they bring value to the world. Focusing on their weaknesses instead of their strengths will not accomplish this. If a child feels valued, then they can develop a sense of belonging, a sense of community, and a sense worthiness. When a child feels that it is safe to be their true authentic self, then their gifts and their purpose can be unwrapped.

> *"Your time is limited, so don't waste it living someone else's life. Don't be trapped by dogma— which is living with the results of other people's thinking. Don't let the noise of others' opinions drown out your own inner voice. And, most important, have the courage to follow your heart and intuition. They somehow already know what you truly want to become."*
> —Steve Jobs

Most of us spend much of our lives wearing one mask or another. Usually, we try on different masks while we are growing up in order to find which one gives us what we are looking for, which is usually the mask that helps us to feel loved, accepted, and a sense of belonging. Once we find that mask, we become habitually attached to it, sometimes even forgetting that it is a mask. But inside, we never feel quite right. There is an internal mismatch of who we are and what we are showing the world. Many of us have experienced this throughout much of our lifetime and spend years as adults trying to find ourselves. We feel unhappy with life choices that don't seem to fit our true selves. We get sucked in to making decisions based on what we think we should be doing, but never truly find the happiness we are searching for. Many of us learn to wear different masks depending on where we are and who we are with, never really being true to who we are.

We learn this pattern early on in our childhood. But what if we felt comfortable from the start just being who we are and never felt as if we had to hide ourselves by wearing a mask? True happiness comes from being comfortable with who we are and not feeling as if we have to hide the truth of ourselves. Helping our children feel comfortable with who they are right from the start is the best way to ensure their genuine happiness in life. When a child feels truly accepted, loved, and a sense of belonging, there is no need for them to try on different masks, and they develop a healthy self-concept. Without a healthy self-concept, it is very hard for a child to feel valued and worthy of all the beautiful gifts, and their inherent gifts might be hidden from the world indefinitely. Without a strong harmonious sense of self, they may continue their search for acceptance until they either find a way to get that need fulfilled or decide to just give up. Not meeting the need of feeling loved and accepted can lead to feelings of despair, anger, and a willingness to do whatever it takes to be seen or heard. The key to true happiness is feeling free to be exactly who you were meant to be with a sense of purpose. Helping our children find this starts with first being aware of these false societal beliefs and then making a conscious decision to love what is. That certainly doesn't mean that we shouldn't help our children be all they can be; at the same time, we need to recognize and honor who they truly are. It has often been said that our children are our greatest resource. This has never been more true than it is today.

When we look back on how society has treated those who appear different, history is full of tragic examples. From the persecution that was carried out in Biblical times to the burning of young women who were believed to practice witchcraft to the genocide in Nazi Germany, there are no shortage of examples of how cruel people can be in the face of "difference." In Steve Silberman's book *NeuroTribes*, the author takes a very in-depth look back at the history of the treatment of individuals with autism and other cognitive differences. In the 1940s, for example, Nazis in Germany sought to purge the world of "feebleminded" individuals by euthanizing institutionalized children. Around this same time, children who exhibited signs of what we now recognize as Asperger's syndrome were taken away from their families and institutionalized in "concealed killing centers" if they weren't deemed high functioning enough. In 1949, Leo Kanner published an article outlining "refrigerator mother syndrome"; he believed children developed autism due to having a cold mother who either neglected or ignored their child and deprived them of warmth and nurture. Bruno Bettelheim gave this idea widespread popularity in the 1950s and 1960s, and many parents suffered greatly from this idea. It wasn't until 1964 that Dr. Bernard Rimland, an American psychologist who had an autistic son, revolutionized our understanding of the autism spectrum with the publication his book *Infantile Autism: The Syndrome and Its Implications for a Neural Theory of Behavior*.

From sterilization practices, electric shock treatments, and institutions, we have made great strides toward creating a world where so many extraordinary individuals who would have historically been treated cruelly now have the opportunity to do extraordinary things. While we have improved our ability to understand and honor the differences that accompany neurodiversity, we still have a long way to go. Today, more and more people are waking up to their inner knowing that there is more than meets the eye. People are hungry for answers that explain more about our feelings and a truth that goes beyond what we have known in the past. At the same time, more and more children are coming into this world to support this new trend. They are coming here with an inner sensory system that is ready for a different type of guidance. The outer circumstances that we have been guided by in the past will not serve our children of the future. An old outdated operating system will not support updated software, just as new wine should not be put into an old wineskin. We are living in a time in which change is happening at a faster pace than ever before, and it is necessary for the survival of humanity that we change as well.

History has shown us that we have already lost many beautiful children, and today beautiful minds are still being lost due to our outdated educational system and our old societal beliefs. In the past couple of decades, we have seen drastic changes in how we see and honor diversity. Interracial marriages, same sex marriages, and transgender acceptance is seen by many of our young people today as all part of the status quo. Our young people are able look past the old societal beliefs when it comes to these issues, because they are following their inner knowing and are not as easily swayed by the old external paradigm. With an empathic view of the world, it is easy to see that everyone plays an important role. From the disabled to our physically strong, from the elderly to our newborn infants, and from the neurotypical to our neurodiverse, everyone is important. We all play an important role in the evolution of humanity.

I truly believe that humanity is headed in a beautiful direction and that our children today are here to guide the way. It is now up to us to change right along with them so that we can see them for the beautiful souls that they are. The evolution of humanity, like the ecosystem, is designed to move us along a continuum toward a more caring, empathic world where everyone is honored for the beautiful soul that they are. Every one of us has beautiful gifts that are unique to our individual wiring. We are all on a journey to unwrap our authenticity and our own unique superpowers. We are all here as a collective, supporting each other in ways that are hard to even imagine. Today's children are tomorrow's answer. As more and more of us wake up to our own empathic heart and see the value of every child and every individual, this world will come together in support of a new paradigm. We are all witnessing a beautiful time in the evolutionary process of humanity. The key is found within the empathic heart of every child, and an empathic heart is the true gift that is found every time a child is unwrapped.

Key Messages: Unwrapping Purpose

» No matter how large or small, strong or weak, outgoing or shy, everyone plays an important role in society.

» Communication is taking place on an energetic level in every moment.

» Lack of understanding about neurological differences among our population causes fear and negative behaviors toward others.

» Everything and everyone are equally important.

» Sensitivity, empathy, and cooperation are all essential to our existence.

» True love is the energy that holds this world together. It comes from the heart and is both internal and eternal.

» Human love comes from the mind and is dependent on outside circumstances and thoughts.

» Our inner needs are equally important if not more important than our physical needs. Our inner needs are needs of the heart.

» Without strong heart-based values, one would not have use of the physical needs, because dying slowly from the inside out can be worse then simply not surviving.

» Not using one's natural-born gifts will wound the spirit.

» Following one's heart will lead them to their own authenticity.

» The key to happiness is feeling free to be exactly who you were meant to be with a sense of purpose.

» Today, more and more people are waking up to their inner knowing that there is more than meets the eye.

» The outer circumstances that we have been guided by in the past will not serve our children of the future.

» With an empathic view of the world, it is easy to see that everyone plays an important role.

CHAPTER 10

Letters from the Heart

"The problem with the world today is that we
are not in our right mind."
—Gandhi

It is time that the old way of being comes to a close, and it is time for a new awakening, which is why so many children today are being born extra sensitive.

Humanity is always evolving, and right now, we are seeing this evolution accelerate. Humanity has always given birth to children who could be described as extra sensitive, but in the past, these children have been the minority, and they were picked on and ridiculed for being different.

Today, this population of sensitive children is exploding. Like popcorn kernels that begin popping one at a time very slowly at first, but then there comes a time when they all start popping, faster and faster, till they are all popped.

That is what we are seeing today. More and more children are being born extra sensitive, and it is our job to help them feel safe, and to help them be who they have come here to be.

There is a special light that shines from the heart of our children and youth today, and we need this light. It's time we help our children shine their light instead of making them feel as if they have to hide it.

I have written this book for all the children who have come here, willing to face the darkness in order to help bring light to the world.

I have written this book for all the courageous parents who have taken on this challenge of raising these children. I want you to know what an important job you have, and I am hoping this book helps you move from frustration, fear, and anger to understanding, hope, and loving what is.

I have written this book for all the teachers, therapists, and school administrators in order to bring understanding, acceptance, and desperately needed change to the way we educate and see our children and youth of today.

And I have written this book for anyone who has ever felt different, has known someone who seems different, or has genuine concern for today's children and youth. It is my hope that this book helps all of us to see each other as important members of society, each with our very own unique set of superpowers just needing to be unwrapped.

As a final note, I have included some letters from the heart.

From a child to Mom and Dad

Dear Mom and Dad,

I know you don't know me yet, but I wanted to write you this letter before I got there so I could just give you a little heads-up. First of all, I want to thank you for accepting this challenge. I know you are going to think that I am not what you thought you were signing up for, but I want to assure you that I will be exactly the way I am supposed to be.

You did sign up for this challenge, and you are going to do a great job! You may question yourself at times, and yes, you will often worry about whether or not you are making the right decisions, but I just want to assure you that every decision you make will be the right one. Even when it appears to be the wrong decision, ultimately there are no wrong decisions. This journey we will be on will have its ups and downs, but we are meant to take it together, and you are going to be the perfect parent for me. As we travel the road of life together, we will be challenged with many obstacles, and together we will grow from each experience.

For example, I may have a teacher one day who doesn't appear to understand me. This is going to frustrate you, and yes, it may even hurt a bit, but together we will teach the teacher kindness. One day, I may come home from school feeling like no one wants to be my friend, but you will be there for me, and you will know exactly what to do and say. I will probably feel very stupid at times, but again, you will be there for me, and whatever you decide to do or say will be perfect. There will be many people who just won't understand me, but you will be there showing me all the love that is in your heart, and together we will teach the world about pure love.

There will be people along the way who will help you. You will not be alone on this journey. Trust in yourself, and trust in the process. Your journey will lead you to all the right people, all the right books, and all the right circumstances. Together, we will make a difference in the world, for that is our function. To teach others pure love through kindness. But since one cannot teach what they have not learned, we will first have to learn from each other.

I am so looking forward to this journey with you, and I really hope that this letter helps. I know it really feels like there are no answers, but I assure you there are, and all will be revealed in Divine time. Just remember, the answer to every problem is love. If you don't completely understand this now, it's okay, it will all make sense to you at the perfect time, and when you understand it, it will be time for you to teach it to me.

Thank you for agreeing to take this journey with me. I truly love you.

Love,

Me

From a parent to themselves

Dear Self,

If you are reading this letter to yourself, then congratulations, you have reached the point where you are ready to know and understand a few things that will be extremely helpful in navigating the rest of your way on this remarkable journey. I want to assure you that you are on the correct path. This is the path you chose, and it is the path most beneficial for your growth and development. You are exactly where you are meant to be, and every circumstance in your life has been exactly what you have needed to get you to where you are today.

I also want you to know that you have never been alone. I have been here with you the entire time, guiding you on your journey, and though you question yourself at times, I am here to assure you that you are doing GREAT! Most importantly, I want to honor you and the courage that you have, to have accepted this very important role in the evolution of humanity. You have accepted the challenge of raising a child who is very important to the world right now.

You see, you are living in a time of great change, and with change comes uncertainty. I know you have surely had a lot of that lately. You have been questioning the meaning behind so many of the challenges that you and your child are having right now, and I know it has been extremely difficult. But I want to assure you that you are on the right path, and you are doing an extraordinary job.

As you know, the world is going through some very difficult times, but that is what is necessary right now in order to bring about the change that is needed, and you, my friend, play a very important role in this change. For you have taken on the courageous challenge of parenting a child who is processing the world differently than most children have in the past. Your child has come into this world with beautiful gifts, and it's time to unwrap them so that the world can truly see what a treasure they are.

Now, I know it doesn't feel like it most of the time, but you are your child's hero, and your child is our hero, and they are here to do extraordinary things. Your child represents a new way of perceiving a world in desperate need of loving kindness, and although you may not have been experiencing much of that lately, I know you will begin to understand this more and more as time goes on. Your child has an extraordinary heart, and it is your job to help them learn how to protect it during these changing times. They are also going to need you to help them recognize their own awesomeness.

This is no easy task, I know, but it is one you chose, and I know you can do it. Together, you and your child will learn from each other, you will support each other, and you will figure this all out. Just remember the key lives in the heart of your child. Their heart is their superpower, and together you and your child will show this to the world. I know you will spend endless hours worrying about them, and you may even find that you have to pull over into a parking lot some days just to have a good cry, but I know you are going to succeed.

Just remember to follow your heart, and let your child lead you to a greater understanding of life and of love. You are on this journey together, and together you will make the change that you, and all of us, are hoping to see in the world.

Thank you, thank you, thank you,

Your Future Self

From a child to a teacher

Dear Teacher,

I just want to thank you for taking on this challenge of being my teacher. I know that it is very hard being a teacher today, and I know you came into this profession wanting to make a difference in the lives of us children. However, being a teacher today is a lot harder than ever before.

You know in your heart how you want to teach me, but you are being told that you have to teach in ways that you know are not in my best interest, and to make matters worse, you have so many children in your class that it is impossible to teach all of us. You also were not properly trained to teach children like me, and this is frustrating you as well. I don't learn the same as everyone else, and my needs are beyond what you are able to provide since there are so many of us in your class.

I know you have a lot of questions, and you want to help me, so I thought I would let you know a little bit about me. First of all, I really do want to learn, and I am capable of learning, it's just that my brain doesn't always process what you are telling me. I often have a hard time keeping up with all the instructions at once. I have a hard time understanding all your words correctly, and once I fall behind your sentence, it's hard for me to catch up and then I just shut down. It's not that I am not paying attention, it's just that there is too much going on in my brain and I get overwhelmed, and I need to turn it off.

I also want you to know that I feel things differently than most children in the past. I feel when you are frustrated with me, and it makes me sad because I don't mean to be so difficult. I feel so different from other children and sometimes I just don't feel like I fit in anywhere. Inside, I know there are so many things I am good at, and I know you would really like me if you got to know me better, but I also know that it's hard for you because of all the policies, restrictions, and expectations that are being placed on you.

You feel judged, and it's not your fault that you are not given the proper environment or the proper tools to teach all of us equally. I know you are doing the best you can, and I just want you to know that I am also doing the best that I can. We are both being put into an environment that is not conducive to teaching for you nor for learning for me. I know change is on its way, but before change, there is always turbulence.

All of the challenges that you and I are facing today is part of the perfect storm that will bring about change. We are both victims of an old paradigm that is no longer serving humanity. Your role in this change is so valuable, and I thank you for your courage to be a teacher during these most challenging times. Your challenges and my challenges are going to bring about this change. It is time to create a new paradigm, and we do know how to do this. We start with creating a new model of cooperation within the classroom. We begin honoring the unique path that each of us are on, and we grow and develop the gifts that each of us are here to share.

The answers that we have all been searching for lie in our hearts. It starts by looking at me through a different set of lenses. It's time that we start looking beyond what our eyes see, and feel what our heart knows. Your heart feels my pain. Your heart can see me, I mean, really see me. Your heart hears me and my cries, and your heart knows who I am. Your heart knows how to celebrate my awesomeness.

My heart aches to be seen and understood, and I just want you to truly know the wonder of me.

With loving kindness and gratitude,

Your student

To all the children and youth of today,

I want you to know how much I honor your courage for coming into the world today during these very turbulent times. I know you probably feel as if you don't belong here, but I want to assure you that you do. You are here to help bring positive change to this world that is desperately in need of what you hold in your heart.

You see, your heart holds the key to unlocking the doors to a new world. The old way of being in this world is no longer supporting humanity, and you are here to bring about the change that we are needing. Yes, I know how hard it is right now to be in this world with such an open and loving heart, and you probably feel the need to close off and protect your heart from this harsh cruelty that surrounds us, but that is not what you are here to do.

You are here to spread loving kindness by feeling the pain and then by releasing it. You see, you weren't just given this strong loving open heart, you were also given the courage that it is going to take to make real change. You were given a strong inner knowing of what is right and what is wrong. You have been given the tools to connect with others and share the power of your loving heart. For you are not in this alone, you are all in this together. Your strengths are your inner senses that connect you with each other and guide you with inner knowledge.

This is extra challenging right now, because most of the world is strongly connected and guided by the external circumstances that surround us, but you, my dear one, are here to change that. You are here to show the world the true strength of inner power. You have the ability to choose what to listen to, the world or your heart. You have the courage to choose which path to take, the one that is well trampled down by the masses or the one less traveled.

True power comes from within, and you have been blessed with an inner guidance system that will lead you and the world away from the old competitive paradigm to a new paradigm based in cooperation. You will use your inner guidance system to connect with others who also hold this gift within their heart, and together you will bring about the change that is needed. Know that you are better together, and together you will accomplish this enormous task. You are not in this alone.

Know that the pain you feel has a purpose, for without struggle and pain there would be no need for change. The challenges you have faced, the hurts you have endured, and the pain that you have felt has all been given to you in order to strengthen your resilience. I know it's been hard, and you question why you feel the pain so deeply, and at times you have felt that you could not go on, but please know that as your heart feels the pain deeply, your heart also has the power to love deeply, and this love is what is going to heal this world.

Your heart has more power than any evil will ever have. Your heart has the capacity to grow and connect with others in a way that this world has never seen before, and with the proper guidance and understanding, you will accomplish what you have come here to do. Inside, you know this is true. The conflict comes from living in a world that is still so strongly attached to external forces, while your inner world knows a different path. The outside world wants you to fall in line and walk the same walk as everyone else, but inside you are being pulled and guided down a path that is still hidden from most.

You have the eyes that can see this new world. You have the ears that can listen to the inner guidance that you are receiving. You have the heart that is capable of feeling the pain of the world, and you have the courage and the knowing to release it. For as you release the pain from your heart, so will the world heal. Know you are not alone, even though it feels that way much of the time. Know that there are those of us who hear your inner cries and have also felt your pain. There are those of us who have walked the path less traveled and we are here to support you.

Know that you are not broken and you don't have to be fixed, for the world is broken, and you are here to help heal the world. Know the difference between power and force. For the external world tries to force change upon us, through judgement, hate, and bullying. You, however, have a heart that holds the power that is stronger than hate, that does not know fear. For the heart knows only love, and love is true power over force. Learn to use the love in your heart to release the pain, and you will accomplish what you have come here to do, and that is to heal the world.

Thank you for being you, for you are exactly who you were meant to be, and you are doing a great job!

With loving kindness and overwhelming gratitude, your friend and colleague,

Shelley

EPILOGUE

One morning in May of 2015 as I meditated in preparation for starting my day, I experienced a vision that led me to write this book. In this vision, I saw a perfect storm. It is hard to explain what that felt like, but at that moment, I knew in my heart without any doubt that I needed to start writing a book. Even though I have never particularly enjoyed writing and have avoided it whenever possible, that morning was different. I could not start writing soon enough, and the words seemed to flow effortlessly. I wrote for most of that day and the next day. The title at the time was "The Perfect Storm" and I thought I was writing a book to help parents understand the challenges they are facing when raising a child who is processing the world differently. I did not know at the time that I was getting ready to live the perfect storm of my life and that my world was about to be turned upside down. I was being guided on an inner journey of transformation that could never have been possible without my perfect storm.

The storm began just a couple of weeks after I started writing. While attending a workshop in California, I tripped and fell and ended up breaking my foot in five places. Now, I know a broken foot seems to hardly qualify as a perfect storm, but it was just the beginning, the distant thunder warning of something much worse to follow. A few weeks later on July 18, 2015, I woke up to a message on my phone telling me that my father had been brutally assaulted in the middle of the night at his nursing home in Texas. I was told that my father had gotten up to use the bathroom, and the resident who lived next door pulled him off the toilet and beat him up. I found out later that this resident had been harassing my father for several weeks and had punched my father in the face while on the toilet just one week earlier. Unfortunately, I had not been told about this incident and there was nothing done to separate this resident from my father.

The results of this incident left my father in what they called an "altered state of consciousness" for two and a half months. There was a significant amount of brain damage, and the doctors had all but given up hope that he would ever recover from his injuries. But the doctors underestimated how stubborn my dad could be, and eventually he began to recover. As we proceeded to look for legal representation to sue the nursing home, we were surprised to learn that it is very difficult to hire an attorney to represent a nursing home abuse case in the state of Texas. State legislation protects nursing homes from being sued by placing a cap on the amount of money that can be claimed in a lawsuit, consequently making it extremely difficult to hire an attorney since there is very little money to be made. Moreover, nursing homes in Texas are ranked 50th in the country for health and safety but are ranked number one in the country when it comes to profitability. This is a huge discrepancy and one that most people are not aware of. I have also been told that there are other states considering adopting this same legislation. In my opinion, this would be a devastating mistake, for my dad's story does not end there.

I knew my father could not stay in that facility, so as he began to recover, we searched for a new nursing home. We found another facility for him to receive rehabilitation; however, it was very difficult to find good care. Although my father was recovering, the quality of care he was receiving in this second nursing home was also disappointing. One morning, as my father lay on the hallway floor awaiting an ambulance to take him to the hospital, he told me the story of how he had fallen. No one had come that morning to take him to breakfast and he was afraid he would miss it, so he ventured out of his room alone. He was just learning how to walk again due to the brain injury and was not very steady on his feet. He was still receiving rehabilitation in order to help him regain the ability to walk and was not supposed to be walking on his own. He fell that morning and broke his hip. This was the beginning of multiple trips to the emergency room, and eventually he passed away in February of 2016, seven months after the initial assault.

During this same time, my mother, who was grieving after my stepfather and her husband of 34 years passed away, decided that she wanted to sell her home and move into my condo in Florida. I flew to Arizona to help her pack up her things and move her across country. I still had my practice of 25 years in Long Island, New York, and I was doing my best to juggle everything in my life. When my father passed away, it became very clear to me that I had to close up my practice and move to Florida to be with my mom. It had been difficult being so far away from my father during this tragic time, and I wanted to make sure nothing like that would happen again with my mom.

I moved to Florida in September 2016, and I am so glad that I did. Just a little over a year later, I took my mother to the doctor because she had awoken abruptly in the middle of the night with a pain in her side. Up until that point, she had been healthy and living independently down the street from me; the day before, she had gone to her favorite nail salon. I can still see her beautiful light blue finger nails as she took her last breath in my living room only one week later.

They found that my mother's liver was full of tumors and they suspected cancer, but she was declining so rapidly that there was not enough time to even get the diagnosis.

We did, however, have a CAT scan done that week, which leads me to another part of this perfect storm that I was living. When my father was assaulted, my desire to write left me. I knew that someday I would finish that book, but with everything going on in my life since then, it just did not feel like the right time. I also knew that I wanted to include in my book something that would help explain why so many children today are feeling so much pain and so much hurt in their heart that they feel as if they have no option other than to walk into a school with a gun. I remember thinking about the Sandy Hook Elementary School shooting in Newtown, Connecticut in 2012, and I wanted to explore that topic in my book.

While my mom and I were at the imaging center for her CAT scan, we heard that there had been another tragic school shooting. This time, it was in our neighborhood at the Marjory Stoneman Douglas High School, right across the street from the imaging center. The following week is still a blur to me as my mom's condition declined rapidly and she passed away only seven days later. I do remember, however, having the realization that everything has its time, and I knew that it was time for me to finish my book. It wasn't until I finished writing the book that I realized the perfect storm I saw during my meditation that morning and the book that I was urged to write were actually for me, because my life was about to become my perfect storm.

What I have learned from all of this is that each one of us truly does hold within our own hearts the gift of resilience. The trick to riding out the storm is to center your heart within the eye. The eye of the storm is quiet and still. It is where our inner senses live. It is our internal strength, our true self. It is the home to our heart. When the external circumstances in our life are flying out of control, we can all get comfort in knowing that within each of our hearts lies the gift of resilience. From the day we are born, we are constantly being bombarded by external stimuli, which is meant to connect us to the physical world. It is during this connection process that most of us lose or simply forget about our inner connections. Scientists are now discovering that our heart contains a neural network similar to our brain and is capable of acting independently from the brain. This allows for two-way communication between the brain and the heart (heartmath.org).

Is it possible that the heart is capable of making connections beyond what our physical senses are capable of making? Could it be that the perfect storm we are living through in this world today is guiding us toward a greater understanding of who we are and what we are truly capable of? When we start to tap into the power of our inner senses and create a strong heart-brain connection, we will then be able to ride out the storms of our lives with ease and grace.

UNWRAPPING RESOURCES

Books

- *The Highly Sensitive Child: Helping Our Children Thrive When the World Overwhelms Them* by Elaine Aron

- *Uncharted: The Journey through Uncertainty to Infinite Possibility* by Colette Baron-Reid

- *When the Brain Can't Hear: Unraveling the Mystery of Auditory Processing Disorder* by Teri James Bellis

- *The Gifts of Imperfection: Let Go of Who You Think You're Supposed to Be and Embrace Who You Are* by Brené Brown

- *Breaking the Habit of Being Yourself: How to Lose Your Mind and Create a New One* by Joe Dispenza

- *Auditory Processing Disorders: Assessment, Management and Treatment* by Donna Geffner and Deborah Ross-Swain

- *The Autistic Brain: Thinking Across the Spectrum* by Temple Grandin

- *Ask* by Ryan Levesque

- *A Theory of Human Motivation* by Abraham Maslow

- *Dying to Be Me: My Journey from Cancer, to Near Death, to True* Healing by Anita Moorjani

- *The Empath's Survival Guide: Life Strategies for Sensitive People* by Judith Orloff

- *A Whole New Mind: Why Right-Brainers Will Rule the Future* by Daniel Pink

- *Your Soul's Plan: Discovering the Real Meaning of the Life You Planned Before You Were Born* by Robert Schwartz

- *NeuroTribes: The Legacy of Autism and the Future of Neurodiversity* by Steve Silberman

- *The Untethered Soul: The Journey Beyond Yourself* by Michael A. Singer

- *It's All God: The Flower and the Fertilizer* by Walter Starcke

- *Tears to Triumph: Spiritual Healing for the Modern Plagues of Anxiety and Depression* by Marianne Williamson

Websites

- projectapproach.org

- peaceliteracy.org

- asha.org